praise for *summertime*

'For anyone who takes comfort in the companionship of animals, the swift grace of birds, the grandeur of trees, the miracle of pollinators and fruitfulness; for anyone who dreads the silence of a lonely, sterile Earth, read this. Now. I'm begging you.'

GERALDINE BROOKS

'*Summertime* deserves to be mentioned in the same breath as other nature-writing classics, such as those by Annie Dillard or Robert Macfarlane. An act of communion not only with animals but with the natural world that sustains us, this book is filled with the spirit of resistance to complacency in the face of catastrophe, and is also an ode to the daily, grounded actions that add up to a realistic politics of care.'

CERIDWEN DOVEY

'Here is a story salvaged from fire, and built from strategic hope, a story of two cherished animals and the lush landscape that Danielle Celermajer hoped to preserve for seven generations. *Summertime* is a rare elegy. It is rich with insights from history and philosophy yet rooted in the radiant detail of everyday life on the land. Vibrant and brave, moving, yet never sentimental, *Summertime* is a passionate call to attend to the worlds we cherish and without which our lives are diminished.'

MIREILLE JUCHAU

DANIELLE CELERMAJER

summertime

REFLECTIONS ON A VANISHING FUTURE

HAMISH HAMILTON
an imprint of
PENGUIN BOOKS

HAMISH HAMILTON

UK | USA | Canada | Ireland | Australia
India | New Zealand | South Africa | China

Hamish Hamilton is part of the Penguin Random House group of companies whose addresses can be found at global.penguinrandomhouse.com

Penguin Random House Australia

First published by Hamish Hamilton in 2021

The epigraph is taken from 'The Eighth Elegy', from *The Essential Rilke,* Hannah Liebmann and Galway Kinnell (trans., ed.)

Cover photograph 'That's Nothing to Laugh About' © Adam Stevenson
Cover design © Penguin Random House Australia Pty Ltd
Typeset in 12/16.5 pt Bembo by Post Pre-press, Brisbane

NATIONAL LIBRARY OF AUSTRALIA
A catalogue record for this book is available from the National Library of Australia

ISBN 978 1 76089 903 5

penguin.com.au

For Katy, for Jimmy and for L, friends all.

contents

after

world

Who has turned us around like this, so that
whatever we do, we find ourselves in the attitude
of someone going away? Just as the person
on the last hill, which shows him his whole valley
one last time, turns, stops, lingers –
so we live, forever taking our leave.

Rainer Maria Rilke, 'The Eighth Elegy'

grief

As I write this on a Friday afternoon it has been forty-eight hours and he has barely lifted his head. We call him, but it is only when we get right up close that he answers, and only in the softest voice – a voice very different from his usual booming baritone. I just climbed down to where he was lying and finally got him to drink a little water, but he showed no interest in food – not even watermelon, his favourite treat. I had no idea that grief could be so deep for anyone.

I have held off telling you that Jimmy is a pig because I appreciate that for many human beings knowing his species would make it impossible to read this as a story about the enormity of loss. But stay with me.

About three years ago a woman who knew that my partner L and I offered refuge to a few animals emailed us to ask if we had space for two pigs who had been rescued from the floor of a factory farm when they were three weeks old. They had been discarded as 'wastage'. For the first six months of their lives Jimmy and Katy were so weak and terrified that it seemed doubtful they would live. But they had huddled by each other's side, and in the love of their human, until they had the strength to enter the world. By the time they came to us at the age of four, they were physically huge but unusually timid. It took about two years before Katy would look at me straight on, and whenever the chickens got into their area, Jimmy – all 200-odd kilograms of him – would scurry away in fear.

On 26 December 2019 the fire that had been edging towards our place was now burning near enough to pose a real threat. When, two days later, I telephoned M, the woman who had raised Jimmy and Katy, to see if she could once again offer them sanctuary, she said she had been half-expecting my call. She would come the next day to take them home, four hours to the south of us, where they could be safe until our place was no longer under threat. The very idea of being 'safe', however, is one of the many casualties of the climate catastrophe. Thirty-six hours later we had not been touched, but a ferocious fire had enveloped M's place, descending upon them from three sides, razing their home, turning the fields to ash, and killing Katy. Given the nature of the fire everyone presumed that Jimmy was also dead. But then, miraculously, just over a day later, Jimmy appeared, having somehow survived an inferno that had vaporised everything else. When I read the first text I received from M, which simply said 'I have found Jimmy', I assumed she had found his body. Moments later a low-quality video followed showing him at a distance next to a burnt-out tree, coming closer and closer till his nose touched the phone camera. The moving image was accompanied by the sound of his snort, a little louder each frame, and M's words, 'I know, I know.'

With roads closed and another catastrophic fire raging through this part of the country only four days after the one that killed Katy, it took us a full week before we could get to Jimmy. A four-hour drive through fire-ravaged country – vaporised forests, flattened homes, empty highways – finally took us to him.

Any fences that would have kept him from running off had been reduced to ash, but after twenty minutes of our calling his name he appeared, pink on the black. He was clearly coming towards us, but he paused about ten metres away and continued as we did, walking in parallel. It was as if the desire to be close could not quite break through the world in which he had been caught. His movements were frenetic. He seemed racked by the hypervigilance he had acquired since his every sense had been assaulted: darkness at dawn; the usual early-morning quiet engulfed in the roar of the flames; the intensity of the colour of the fire; the radiant heat that, a week later, still emanated from the ground; the taste of ash. This sensory apocalypse had come upon Jimmy out of nowhere; how could he possibly know when it would return?

After we got Jimmy home he shuffled over to his mud bath and lowered his huge, hot, shaken body into it. We were overcome with joy as we watched him rediscover the possibility of coolness. He ate watermelon and drank cold water and slept. But he slept alone, not, as he had every night of his life before the fire, next to Katy.

The next morning he began to look for her. Everywhere. In their house, down in their woods, up under the trees where they had once taken shade from the afternoon sun. He would turn and look and stand very still – listening for her, perhaps smelling the remnants of her presence. And then he stopped. My guess is that now he was home he felt he could cease being hypervigilant. He could relax the terror that had been keeping him in movement. But with that relaxation both the reality of Katy's death and the trauma of his experience of the fire came to the fore. He placed his body on the cool of the earth, and there he remained. When he will get up again, and whether he will find a way back to his world, are among the uncertainties we now have to live with.

I went and sat alone, just down the slope from where Jimmy has been lying. It is way down in the bush over a gully. The light is soft; you can hear the birds and the wind moving through the trees. The air and the earth are cool, and the smell is of leaves and the river. I cannot presume to know what he is doing when he lies there, but it seems that he is taking himself back to an ecology not wrought by the terror of the fires, nor fuelled by our violence on the earth. He is letting another earth heal him.

When people speak about the fires they often speak about being overwhelmed by the enormity of the devastation. We do not really have the capacity to grasp this much loss – not only to humans, but to other wild and domesticated animals, to the bush, to the ecologies of rivers and moss and the creatures who flourish there, to the possibility of regeneration. I know I don't. But I can hold Jimmy's enormous grieving head in my arms and be present to the gravity and finality of this loss. And, at the same time, to his broken but miraculous presence.

before

presence

We had not even come through the gate that marks the beginning of 'the property' before I knew this place was where I wanted to stay, to live, to be. I stepped out of the car to open the gate to let the others drive through, then closed it, waved them on, and walked down the dirt drive towards the old white farmhouse that was peering out from behind a high hedge on my left. On the other side of the drive from the house, two horses – one black, but flecked white in his old age, and one chestnut – lifted their heads from where they were grazing in a small paddock, considered me, and went back to the grass. At the end of their paddock, just over the old moss-covered wooden fence, I could see a small orchard, the vestiges of the blossoms of the early spring – apple, pear and almond – still evident.

The real estate agent wanted L and I to drive with him through the land so he could show us the river. It was not just that I wanted to walk. I wanted to take off my shoes and feel my feet on the earth and the earth on my feet. L and I declined the offer and walked, albeit with shoes on. We followed the drive away from the front gate, past the horses and the orchard on one side, and a pond frequented by wood ducks on the other, till the road narrowed where an old stone wall came to what had once been the milking shed.

Through another gate we entered a large open field, flanked on one side by huge gums, acacias, wattle trees and cedars, and on the other by a steep slope that fell towards the pastures below. At the bottom of the field we came to an old blue corrugated-iron shed, open on three sides, with a rusted water tank tacked onto the roof to collect the rainwater. From there we followed the path the horses had worn as they moved through their days, skirting the dense rainforest to the north, down the hill, and at that point turning back in the direction from which we had come and out into another large paddock that opened up beneath the house.

I have a photo I took from there on that day, looking over the deep spring green of the pasture, the darkening trees of the rainforest and up to the escarpments that rise to the west from the other side of the river that lay below. When you stand in that spot, in every direction you are held by the land: escarpments tight around you to the east and west, the valley closing in on itself to the north, and, to the south, vast stretches of rainforest that have resumed their presence in this landscape during the sixty-odd years since anyone farmed here and that now create a dense blanket between you and the escarpments visible in the distance further south. It was late morning the first time I stood there, but in the mid to late afternoon, if the sun is at the right angle, the rockface of those distant giants glows orange back at you.

In the reflection of their presence it is possible to feel a sense of permanence, safety amid all that is transient and mortal. I remember the first time I fell deeply and completely in love. Barely a breath after love arrived terror; the realisation that the one whom I loved would one day pass out of existence. But here, I then believed, was love assured of permanence. Not mine, but of this place.

You might guess that having escaped the real estate agent's earshot L and I would have taken the opportunity to speak about our impressions, but there was no need. Besides, there were magpies, currawongs, rock warblers, eastern whipbirds, and king parrots to listen to – not that I recognised their distinct sounds then.

When we came to the far end of the paddock below the house, we climbed, more gingerly now, down the steep rocky road that winds its way through the dense rainforest, until eventually we emerged from the darkness of the canopy out into the large pasture at the bottom of the hill. Almost a circle, open to the sky, enfolded by thick woods. The real estate agent, leaning on his Range Rover parked in the far corner of the field, hollered out for us to come over. When we got there he ushered us down a steep walking trail marked by poles stuck in the ground topped with plastic yellow caps, thick moist leaf underfoot, and makeshift stairs occasionally breaking the slipperiness of the slope. We could hear the river long before we caught sight of it. When we came upon it at the bottom of the trail the source of the sound made itself known. Not simply the river flowing, but a waterfall, approximately three metres high. From the sequence of pools, the water gathered momentarily as it swirled through the eddies then tumbled in a racket to the waterhole below. A perfect pool, held on all sides by boulders fallen from the escarpments that towered above us on the far side of the river. Even without touching it, the absence of light and the darkness of the water betraying its evident depth told you it was cold. I crouched down, stuck my hands in one of the pools and threw the water up, jewels in the air, and then back on my face.

The spray coming off moving water, the light from forest, the sounds of river moving through rocks and between pools, the smell of moss; they enveloped me. In moments like these, moments of astonishing beauty, you can slip into feeling like you are in a picture that rises up from your memory, or one that you are already imagining you will later recollect and share with others in the form of a story. But the thickness of it all held me right there in the real. Presence.

On occasions, the expression 'left an impression' can flee the world of metaphor and return to the literal that perhaps it once was, as if there is an indentation in your skin where you have been marked. We returned to the land the following week, this time alone, to give that impression the time to press itself more deeply into our skin, our flesh, our bones. We pushed our bodies through what had once been pastures but were now overgrown, thick with ferns, until we came upon a stream that ran down into the main river, the water seeping under huge moss-covered boulders, reappearing and resuming its flow until it hit the next cluster of rocks and disappeared again. We discovered the skeleton of a horse in a ravine that drops down to the river. In the late afternoon we trekked up the steep road that leads from the house to the top pasture and watched storm clouds darkening the escarpments. As the first drops began to fall on us, I turned to L and told him that this was where I wanted to die.

I remember walking under the canopy that the trees create along the road, pondering the strangeness of 'buying' the land and the oddness of 'price'. Within the world of the real estate market land is worth as much as people are willing to pay for it; its value is an entirely comparative and competitive artefact. But what about the value of the life this place could open up for us and the others (human and other-than-human) with whom we could share that life? What about the land's intrinsic value, one that cannot be tagged against any currency or measured by any metric, one that does not change over time because it has no quantity? What about its value understood as the life, presence and relationships of all the beings that make the place what it is: the rainforest, the animals, the river, the shifting light on the escarpments? And what about the value and meaning this place once had (and still has) for the Aboriginal peoples for whom it was and is Country? What of the thick relationship between traditional custodians and place, which we – the settler colonial society – have decimated, leaving nothing but the name of the river, recalling an Aboriginal man we killed?

It is an idea often associated with Indigenous peoples, that it is humans who belong to Country and not the other way around. That we humans cannot own land but are only ever its custodians, a duty that we can both observe and abuse. Walking through the land, listening to the river, feeling the cool come in as the light drew away from the escarpments in the late afternoon, there was nothing culturally remote or abstract about that way of understanding the relationship. What felt alien was the idea that what enveloped me, what held me up as I stood there, was 'property' that we might 'own'. True, there is no getting away from the fact that this property paradigm is the way that we humans (or at least those who get to make the rules) have come to organise the planet and pretty much everything on it. There is no denying the power it invests in some people to keep others – people and other beings – out. And where our presence is pervasive, where we have covered the land with concrete and bitumen, levelled it, ploughed and planted it, changed the direction of the water so it runs through pipes we have dug into the ground, blocked the movement of the light and the shifts in temperature so we can adjust them according to our comfort, it is easy to become convinced that it is all here for us.

Yet still, you might find yourself in the presence of a world where water moves around boulders that fell from the escarpments before the first human word had been spoken, where the light shifts and temperatures change according to the movement of days and seasons that turn and turn in our absence. Then that paradigm, for all its tenacity, starts to fade. You start to experience it as nothing more than the thinnest, flimsiest of films that has been laid (often violently) over place. The bitter irony is that while we humans are the only ones convinced by it, it is a paradigm that has afforded us the capacity to alter, and perhaps even to kill, everything.

It would be a mistake to believe that the way we understand the world is simply an idea, and one we might change just as we change our minds about people we once did not like but now do.

Understandings, those achievements we feel so proud of as humans, are also shaped by the world in which we are emplaced. Up until this time I had lived almost all of my life in places where it was easy to be convinced by the paradigm I just described. So convinced, in fact, that it did not seem like a paradigm at all; just a description of reality. But I had also begun to recognise that the more convinced we are by this curious way of making sense of the world, the more we feel entitled to transform that world, in all its otherness, into something we can tell ourselves we own. And so on we go, until more and more of the world becomes thus, imbued with the signs of our presence. We make an impression.

The idea that I could will or think myself into another way of understanding, that it was up to me to decide what type of relationship I was going to form with the world, was more of the same fantasy: that I, the human, was so powerful I could change how the world occurred to me and, hence, our relationship. Thankfully there is still a wisdom, a worldliness, in us that has us know otherwise. Or perhaps a perceptual capacity that is yet to be called forth. If our relationship with other beings and our shared home was going to change, those still more powerful than me needed to guide the process.

My part was to take myself to a place where the old conceit could not sustain itself. Where it would not be me working on the earth to make her mine – or even to make me hers – but the earth working on me to make of me, and of us, what she still could.

futures

The light that falls through the rainforest is always mottled. By the time it reaches you it has passed through the layers of the leaves and vines, the branches and trunks that fold and twist over and among each other. The humus and leaf litter are soft and moist underfoot because the light that reaches them is muted. They stew down there in the wet, and are thick with insects, worms and new ferns just emerging like green beetles. When it has been raining, some of the fungi that grow on the forest floor seem implausible. In the first year we were here I photographed an extraordinary form that was larger than a tall man's boot, bright orange and porous like a sea sponge. Last year, I walked down the slope to the place where the mushrooms used to grow and the earth smelt dank. Now the leaves crackled beneath my boots. There was no give in the earth.

Down where the rainforest slopes towards the river there is a grove of huge trees, their ochre trunks reaching high above the canopy. It hurts your neck to try to see their upper branches. There is one whose trunk must have a diameter of three metres at least. You'd need a good eight people, arms outstretched and holding hands, to encircle it. He is remarkable and when you see him he stops you in your tracks. He is also, quite evidently, part of a larger multigenerational family, not only of the trees of the same species but also of creepers, bird's nest ferns, other trees, the animals and insects that live in and on him, and the mycelium that stretches beneath and among them. Even when he dies he will continue to nurture this community. The hollows that form in his trunk will be homes for small marsupials such as bush rats, possums and antechinuses; for bats and gliders; goannas; frogs and snakes; parrots and owls. The decaying wood will provide habitat, breeding grounds and food for beetles, ants, worms and snails. Those wondrous orange parasites that catch your eye when you walk through the forest will form a line along his body when he eventually lies horizontal.

And as they all do this they will transform what he has become into nutrients in and on the forest floor, from which others will grow. I named the tree Isaac.

Isaac was my grandfather. He came on a boat to Australia with Hela, my grandmother, and John, my father, in April 1950. Right after the end of the war, they fled from Poland to Paris, and it was from there that they obtained refugee status and a passage to Australia. Other than Hela and John no one from Isaac's family survived the war. He told me that his business partner had escaped to Argentina, where he changed his family name from Zając, Polish for hare, to Królik, which means rabbit. Or perhaps it was the other way around. Isaac and Hela's daughter, my father's sister, Alma, was taken by the Gestapo in 1942 when the family was in hiding in Warsaw, and murdered. She was twelve.

When the three of them arrived in Australia with barely a word of English, they virtually stopped speaking their native tongue. Their lives were, and, I came to understand, had to be, about the future. As he had learned from his Jewish forebears, everything that Isaac did was oriented towards the community he felt part of, and to the lives of his grandchildren, and their children – down seven generations. People who did not yet exist, and whom he would never know, but whose yet-to-be lives guided his. It is one of the human qualities that takes your breath away, this capacity to be consciously present not only to what you might make from what is immediately in front of you in time and space, but to what that could become, long after you are gone. We continue to draw nourishment from the spring he opened.

When I turned fifty it occurred to me that it was my turn to live towards seven generations. It sounds like a romantic idea, but when you actually go about realising it you start to fathom the difficulty of the task – to orient yourself, and to start to act in ways that are given by your care for future lives whose context and shape will always remain opaque to you. It means imagining not only what those lives might be like, but what nourishment they might most need. And even if you have a model to inspire you, as I did in Isaac, your time is not their time. 2014 was not 1950.

When I tried to look forward, to *feel* forward, what seemed most vital was access to fertile land and sources of clean water. And, along with that, lifeways and understandings that would have those seven generations feel at home on, delighted by, grateful for and responsible to the earth and the other beings who supported and accompanied them. That is what had us find our way to this valley, and that is why the most magnificent tree in our midst bears the name Isaac.

Around me I hear whisperings, almost shamefully spoken, of people's fear for the future. Since the fires began to consume the worlds around us, the reverberations of those whisperings have intensified. People have started to use the term 'existential threat' to convey the idea that not just human lives but human *life* is at stake. It is not inaccurate, but it does not quite make present or bring close what is happening in our bodies as we sense this peril. Maybe it is easier to adopt an abstract idiom than to speak out loud about the intimate, palpable and direct losses we would prefer not to name. Maybe we believe that if we don't give them shape in the form of words, they will vanish. Or maybe we are trying to shield ourselves from the flood of feelings they would elicit.

But it is only fantastical thinking that has you believe that silence will stop the dreaded future from coming to pass. I'd hazard a guess that wrapping words around our still-amorphous feelings, and giving voice to the ones we already know we harbour, might be a corner piece in the puzzle of learning how to live in this world. If we are to have any chance of mitigating that dreaded future, difficult actions lie before us. Speaking the feared future, and being present with each other to how desperately we do not want it, may give us the clarity and resolve we need to act. And if or when it is too late for such actions, if there is no more to be done to prevent that future, honesty will be the only solid ground on which to stand. To stand and hold on to each other.

Sometimes I take a walk to visit Isaac. He is good for being straight with. These last few years, through the work of scientists, novelists and artists, we have learned so much more about trees than we in the West have ever allowed ourselves to acknowledge before, so I would not presume even to guess what capacity he has to 'know' about the future. It took us suspending our certainties about the order of life for long enough to pay attention to trees as something other than resource, aesthetic object or environment for (other) sentient life. Already we have learned that they communicate with each other about drought or disease or harmful predators using chemical, hormonal and slow-pulsing electrical signals. They know, and share with each other what they know, about what might threaten them. I'd hazard a guess they also know, and share what they know, about what pleases them.

I wonder what Isaac has come to know, both in these last years, as the temperature he lives in has risen and the rainfall has declined, and now, as the fire that is approaching has already killed others like him who lived in the millions of hectares that form his larger home. I wonder whether Isaac has received the message that others' immediate worlds are disappearing as the fires move from root to crown, from leaf litter to fungi to trunks to leaves to birds. I wonder how Isaac, who by his nature orients his life to seven generations, looks to the future now.

cycles

We think weather is something that comes down onto the planet, but living here I have discovered that it is much more relational than that. Where there is rainforest there is also rain – not just because the rain makes the forest but because the forest makes the rain. High beneath the escarpments that slope down to the river, this valley is blessed, or, perhaps better, has been blessed, with cool weather. Even when the temperature reached 40 degrees in town it would stay below 35 here, even milder if you walked down to the river and sat on the mossy rocks where the sun peeks through the narrow break in the canopy for only a couple of hours a day. Slip into and out of the river and you can stay around for hours, relatively unbothered by the brutal heat beating down everywhere else. Even on the hottest days, Jimmy and Katy could cover themselves in mud and head down into the forested area at the bottom of their world, sinking down into the dirt that remains cool beneath the trees, and rest until the afternoon breeze woke them.

A couple of summers back, L and I convinced some friends, who were new to Australia and sweltering in their rented home just to the north, to come to the valley. The five of us spent the day lolling around the river until the late afternoon hours. They were delighted by the relief that the river and the rainforest offered, but later freaked out when the bloodstains all over the kitchen floor alerted them to the leeches that had attached themselves to their ankles and lower legs. It's not that I'm keen on those black suckers, but they come, quite literally, with the territory. Cool and damp and leechy. Two years later I've not seen a single leech all summer. Funny what you start to miss.

But today has put paid to the rule of 'cooler up here'. The predictions are alarming. The temperature is expected to reach 44 degrees. The fire conditions are catastrophic, meaning that if a fire starts it will annihilate whatever sits in its path. Neither the houses Australians have been carefully designing and building during these fire-prone years, nor those Australian ecosystems uniquely adapted to thrive on fire can withstand the types of fires that burn under catastrophic conditions. But when L tells me to come and take a look at the temperature gauge he's placed on the deck, which is coming in at 46.5 degrees, I assume he is reading it incorrectly. Just another instance of choosing the option 'the facts must be wrong' over the option 'face the facts'. When I see for myself that he has not got the facts wrong I assume it is because atmospheric temperatures need to be taken in the shade not the sun. I pick up the gauge from the chair where it has been sitting and carry chair and gauge around to the other side of the house where the shade is falling. I place them, chair and then gauge, in the proper location to take a temperature. The shade. I stroll back inside, knowingly. Twenty minutes later I go out to check. 46.5 degrees.

It is a dangerous day for this type of heat, with two fires burning and shifting their ground at emergency level, still some distance away, but not *that* far to the south. If even a single stray ember from one of those fires flies out in front of it, or if dry lightning strikes a tree or leaf litter, now desiccated from years without rain, those fires will skip over the buffer zones that lie between us and them. And they will rip through this land with the uncompromising potency they have already shown themselves capable of when they visited their force upon the lands and their inhabitants to our north, south and west. A few people have already left the valley, and the rest of us are primed to go; fire emergency kit in the front bedroom or already in the car. Clothes to cover every part of your body against the heat of the flames, wool blankets to protect your body if flames pass over, torches to help you make your way through the dark that descends in the middle of the day, a chainsaw to cut a fallen branch blocking your way to escape, water to quell your parched and panicked body. L remarks how lucky we are that most people have stopped smoking in their cars. One cigarette tossed out a window – that'd be it.

A few weeks ago, realising how underprepared we were for reality as it was unfolding, I followed up on a note a neighbour had sent and called the woman from the Rural Fire Service who had offered to come up to people's places to advise on how best to prepare the land and protect the animals. When the fires started in the north we initially retained our faith that, because we lived in the rainforest, we would be safe. When you walk in the bush here, there are no signs of past fires – no darkened trunks, no altered patterns of growth betraying the mark a fire once made. But then the rainforests in the north started to burn, and with them the security of my faith in our being protected.

I can easily bring to my mind's eye a scene laid bare in a short clip posted on social media: the camera is panning across the charred, empty land. Now it moves its gaze into the shell that was once home for the person holding the camera and back out across the treeless landscape. Right beside it is an older film of the world before the fire: the astonishing beauty of myriad rainforest greens, the movement of the birds in and out of forests that are no longer there. The sense of permanence that grounded my love of this place shook like the hand of the man taking the film.

L and I and the woman from the RFS walked around the land together so she could get a sense of the risks and how we might best manage them. When we stopped I could see her surveying the thick bush within which are huddled the small open spaces where we and the animals live. When she spoke the words, 'It's not a matter of *if*, but only of *when*,' it probably looked to her (and maybe even to L) as if I was still standing in the paddock listening.

But I was actually trying to still myself against the cacophony in my head: a screaming match between panic and 'the facts must be wrong'.

We explained to her that we did not have the means to evacuate all of the animals in the event of a fire – we had no truck, no float, and, more importantly, no ability to get the donkeys onto a truck. Maybe Jimmy and Katy would follow us if we had a bucket of carrots, but I could hardly be confident. The vision of how I wanted us to live here paid homage to Thoreau's maxim: 'a man [sic] is rich in proportion to the number of things which he can afford to let alone'. My version entailed not 'training' any of the animals, letting them move across the land according to their own rhythms, respecting their choice to approach or withdraw. A fine sentiment so long as you assume that the world is not about to become an inferno. When letting them alone becomes letting them alone to conditions they cannot survive, is that still love?

On the advice of the RFS expert we picked out the best pastures in which to place all the animals, should it look like a fire was approaching. One for the horses and donkeys. One for the sheep, the goats and the pigs. They were the ones with the fewest trees or bushes that could go up, but that were still big enough that, if a fire passed through, the animals could move to the side where it wasn't yet burning and then back to the side where it had already burnt. I found myself trying to imagine how they would do that without going through the fire. Or, to put that another way, I imagined them going through the flames.

The problem was that the ideal pasture for the donkeys and horses was also the one where we kept huge piles of wood that we collect over the course of the year for the bonfire that L and the kids build to burn at our annual winter solstice gathering. Every year, as we move from autumn into winter, they make a more elaborate structure that goes up in flames on the longest night of the year. It has become a poignant symbol for us of the earth's movement from the darkness of the short days back into the light. Our neighbours, friends and family gather around it every year to remind ourselves of the cycles we can rely on. That no matter what we do there will be a lengthening of the times of darkness followed by a return to the light.

This summer I started to hate that wood. I made L drop everything he was doing until every pile had been moved, either out of the pastures altogether or over to one side by the woods, so it would not provide a stepping stone for the fire to leap across from one part of the bush to the other. There will be no bonfire this winter. From where I stand now it is incomprehensible that fire could feel welcoming.

It will not be long till we revise the part of our fire plan that says to move the animals into the 'safe pastures' if it looks like a fire is going to reach here. That was based on the old belief that cleared land is safe from fire. A few weeks of watching what has been happening elsewhere makes the folly of the belief – and hence the plan – apparent. People are coming to see that the conflagrations we have made are so fierce that they can burn on oxygen alone: no trees required. You'd think that the old belief would be among the casualties of these fires, but it serves to sustain the fantasy that the more we clear the land of trees, the safer we will be. As if we could, and should, live immunised from the dangers that other beings pose to our sovereign realm: trees that might burn, animals that might contaminate. Even if the flames did not burn through the cleared land, the animals would be left in the middle of hundreds of hectares of blazing or smouldering bushland. The dense smoke, the loss of oxygen, or the radiant heat would kill them. But on this 46.5-degree day we have not come to that point of recognition. We are still naive and hopeful, and so late yesterday evening we moved everyone into their 'safe' paddocks in case the fire made its way through the night, showing up in the early hours of the morning before we were ready.

Two, three and four in the afternoon, and the temperature is still up above 45 degrees. Around 4.30 the wind starts to come up. Nowadays I have come to feel genuine ambivalence towards the afternoon southerlies that have long been a part of Australian summers. Perhaps it will cool things down. Perhaps it will whip the fire up. By around 5.30 I have come down on the side of liking this wind. No new fires have started near us. I check the Rural Fire Service's Fires Near Me app. You open it and a map of the state appears. Wherever there is an active fire, the site is marked by a coloured icon: blue for advice – there is a fire there; yellow for watch and act – monitor and be ready to take action; red for emergency – leave if it's not too late. The icon on the map over the fire to the south has gone from red back to yellow. The other fire, yet further south, has moved away towards the west. The temperature has dropped, and when I go outside my body feels good.

I look out the window and catch sight of the donkeys in the paddock by the house. Ingenious ratbags, they have either opened the slightly makeshift gate we had put up in a rush last night, or perhaps they orienteered their way down through the bush to where you can sneak around the fence and back into the 'unsafe' pastures. But now that the temperature is in the twenties and the icon is yellow, I can relish their resourcefulness.

About half an hour later I look outside again. To the south-west, the sky is a colour I have not seen before. All this summer, the skies have moved through a series of uncanny palettes. The phrase, 'it looks like we are on another planet' has become a regular feature of conversations. But this sky is different again. Black-red. I cannot make out the flames that are surely the source of this thickened light but I sense their presence beyond the escarpments that hold their arms around this valley. I go to my phone to check the Fires Near Me app again. The icon floating above the fire just to the south has changed from yellow to red. I turn on the radio. I start checking the Facebook groups. In moments like these, when the changes are so rapid and the conditions so unpredictable, it is difficult to get accurate information. To the best I can find out it seems that a pyrocumulus cloud has formed over the fire burning to our south. From where I am standing and watching it *appears* as if a storm is approaching, and this raw perception, unmediated by thought, immediately makes me feel better. My body encodes the apparently logical association between the visual impression of a thick dark cloud and the sound and feeling of rain. The sensual relief lasts for the split second it takes for my updated mind to reassert itself over my body's outdated systems of knowing. This is a different type of storm – a storm that produces dry lightning not rainstorm lightning. What falls from the clouds is ash-rain, not water-rain. Windowsills, people's cars, the vegetables in the garden, your clothes if you left them on the line, all strewn with black or dirty-grey ash. It is as if some malevolent demon from one of the eastern European fairy tales my mother used to read to my brother and me when we were little has materialised. Dressed in silk, speaks in a sweet voice and looks like it is here to help you. And then it gobbles you up, sometimes cooking you first. Has the appearance of clouds, darkens the sky, and looks like it will bring the rain you are aching for. And then it starts more fire. The weather system creates a fire that creates a weather system that creates more fire.

Feedback loops. Our school mathematics ill-prepare us to grasp these non-linear patterns of accelerating disaster. Almost every chart or graph that most of us have seen shows a continuous line moving upwards or downwards, or flatlining. Historically scientists have constructed graphs like those by collecting data on how a certain variable has behaved in the past – say, the temperatures every year for the last 500 years – and charted the data points so that a trained eye can detect a pattern and then represent that pattern as a line with a certain gradient or slope. The line tells us that, over time, that variable (temperature, rainfall, price and so on) is going up or going down, at this rate or at a changing rate, and so on. Then they project that line into a future that we cannot yet measure because it has not yet happened. The line extends out beyond what we currently know and where we currently stand, but the patterning of the past assures us of a certain predictability into the future to come.

Of course we also know that new causal factors that were not part of the picture of the past can enter the scene and change the course of the future. If researchers know that new variables are going to be introduced into the system they need to do their best to factor those into the gradient of the line. For example, if you are trying to work out what your future earnings might look like you would plot your past earnings and project the line forward. But if you work in a sector that is dependent on a certain raw material that is fast running out with no replacement in sight, or if you know that demand for what you produce is rapidly disappearing, perhaps because of some other environmental disaster, disease or financial crisis, you would need to factor that in to get a realistic picture of the most likely future. By the same token, if we know that carbon in the atmosphere causes increases in temperature and we know that every year we are going to be pumping out more and more carbon, we need to factor that in to the change in the gradient of the line. Although it might take some concentration to model the moving parts – especially for those of us who thought maths stopped with the end of school – the logic of cause and effect is one that makes sense to us.

But then something else happens. Changes that are effects themselves become causes of other effects, and even new causes of the factors that initially caused *them*. All within complex interacting systems. Here is one. We think of sea ice – the frozen continents or the glaciers – as critically important in stabilising global temperatures, most obviously because their own frigid temperatures keep the world around them cool (think of wind passing over ice: air conditioning!), and because so long as they are frozen, sea levels will remain reasonably stable. They also matter because they are bright white, so when the sun hits them, instead of staying in the atmosphere the heat bounces back up. When atmospheric and, even more importantly, ocean temperatures rise because of increases in the concentration of carbon, the ice starts to melt. The immediate impact is that the beneficial effects of ice are removed from the climatic system. But not only that – where there was white, reflective ice, there is now dark land or ocean. Dark that absorbs the heat, causing more ice to melt. At the same time the methane, which was harmless as long as it was trapped in the ice, starts to be released from the melting ice. Once unfrozen, methane starts to act as another greenhouse gas, contributing to warming, to melting, to warming . . . you get the picture.

It is difficult to get your head around the game of causality here, especially when panic sets in, and whatever remnant mathematical capacities we have start to disintegrate. What really does your head in is how this picture now oscillates between what humans are causing and the cascade of causes that escape our control. The data indicate that it is us and our actions behind all of these shifts: we burn fossil fuels that increase the atmospheric carbon and we cut down the trees that would have taken carbon out of the atmosphere. The resultant increases in atmospheric carbon produce climate changes, which show up as fires, as droughts, as tornadoes, and as rising sea levels.

But then those changes that we wrought start to take off on their own, outpacing any line we might project into the future. I am back to my fairy tales. In our curiosity and absurd confidence in our own invulnerability we opened the closet door, or snuck the box out from its hiding place beneath the floor. Out leapt the demon. Bad enough, but nothing like the demons begotten by the demon. And now our door-closing or box-replacing abilities are worthless.

What is worse? To feel ashamed at the havoc we have wreaked but still be at the centre of the world, the agent making all of this happen? Or to be the panicked, impotent witness, outstripped by new agencies altering the world largely on their own?

This evening temperatures are back down to tolerable. We had thought that the combined effect of human efforts and a fortuitous change in the 'weather' had tamed the fire to a point where we, or at least the humans looking after us, had some type of control. But then the fire unleashed its own creative capacities. Its own weather. My amusement at the donkeys' having escaped the safe pasture was based on a naive miscalculation. Mine was a linear graph that factored in a bunch of causes: temperatures, winds, dryness, human efforts. But I had forgotten to factor in the new agents and relationships that now accompany us on this planet and are making their own curves. Us, the fire, the fire's storm, the dry lightning, the fire.

Now rattled, we go outside to send the donkeys back into their 'safe' pasture. It is cool, but the whole sky is now the colour of an old bruise – purple-brown – and you can't escape the eeriness. I say a quiet thanks because the donkeys are now hanging out close by the gate. I open it, chase them in, and shut it behind them. We walk away.

There is a break in the smoke and the fire's clouds, and we find ourselves standing under the blue of evening sky. For a few moments, but only a very few, the light breaks through my thoughts and I have that simple feeling that it is all okay again. That the darkness has given way to light and we can rest in that ancient faith in cycles that settle, eventually, into a flatline across time.

attention

On any other summer morning, if the day is calm and you happen to be in the right spot, you can see seven donkeys moseying along a trail that passes just below the house. They are done with their preferred early morning activities – chilling under the chestnut trees, grazing behind the vegetable garden, checking Jimmy and Katy out over the fence, loitering by the side of the house and looking expectantly into our kitchen. Responding to some type of signal that I have never quite been able to make out – the angle of the sun, or a shift in the temperature – they are heading out for their day.

If they sense that it is going to be a hot one they might disappear through a break between the trees, down the steep path that winds through the rainforest to the lower pasture. It is always a few degrees cooler nearer the river, and we might not see them again until the heat of the day eases in the mid-afternoon, when they trek back up to the old stone trough in the upper pasture. If the day is mild, instead of heading down to the lower part of the land, they might keep going past the house and over to the horses' stables, where they pause, and then saunter out into the paddock that opens before them to eat and sleep and play. As they make their way out, they form a ragtag but unmistakable line, never more than few metres apart from each other – everyone except for Puzzle, who is just as likely to have missed the signal and then not noticed that they have left. Until, that is, he emerges from his daydream, looks up, and discovers he is alone.

Puzzle was among the first of the animals to come to live here with us. The day he was due to arrive on the truck that was bringing him down from Queensland I had to be in the city, so I was on the phone every half hour to L to check if Puzzle had arrived. I'd implored the truck driver, who clearly thought I was a little unhinged, to make sure there was some sponge or soft fabric stuck to the inside back of the truck so that in the anxiety of the journey

Puzzle did not rub himself raw. L reported that when he stepped out of the truck Puzzle seemed fazed from two days' travel and that the hair on his backside had been rubbed right off, exposing inflamed skin, but when he walked into the garden he lay down and gazed out over the valley. When I arrived home a few hours later I found him still there, his huge, grey, slightly bony body on the deep green grass just beneath the lemon tree by the back door of the house.

He seemed unperturbed by the presence of strangers (us) or by the unfamiliar landscape – its smells, its sounds, the quality of the light. Having lived his entire adult life alone, or with horses who did not want a bar of him, he even seemed to find an understated comfort in the presence of Zach, the baby donkey whose company he now kept. But his default relationship with the world soon became clear: *worry*. If we tried to spray fly repellent on his legs, or to rub ointment into his black skin where insects had bitten through the thin white hair, he regarded us with grave suspicion. When the farrier tried to pick up his feet to trim his hoofs he clearly anticipated grievous bodily harm. In that first month of his being here the rains were torrential. I would lie in bed listening to the thick drops on the roof, knowing that the two of them would be standing out there, ears horizontal, soaked through, miserable. Inevitably L and I would get up, don our raincoats and gumboots, and coax him, or more likely drag him, into the shelter of the old milking shed.

And yet on clear nights when we walked out to take in the darkened land, it was Puzzle who had placed himself so that from where he lay he could tilt his head to look over the valley and gaze out to the stars. It was Puzzle who seemed to contemplate what unfolded before him in wonder, always offering me that possibility of looking at the stars as if – to paraphrase the poet Joseph Brodsky – I did not know the names of the constellations.

In the 'social' realm it took a good couple of years for things to shift for Puzzle. Donkeys, like people, have firm views about how the world works, and habits of life that cement those views in place. They settle on the likely sequence of events and the feelings they are likely to elicit, and they tend to be highly resistant to letting contradictory evidence shift their expectations. We call them stubborn, but if we were not so dogged about that habit of thought we might consider that what they are doing is working with the map *they* have constructed for themselves to navigate the world, placing more trust in that than in what the human is suggesting they ought to do.

They stick with their own map tenaciously, staring down at its coordinates so that any new evidence that might reveal its flaws has a hard time attracting their attention. And that remains the case, even if the ways they are currently living are not that great, considered from a broader perspective. Even if the world changes around them. Even if the evidence suggests they should change.

Eventually Puzzle figured out that he had the wrong map for the world he was now living in. If, through force or patient persuasion, the people (again, that's us) actually managed to get away with the strange things that they wanted to do to him, it turned out that the disasters he had foreseen did not transpire after all. Quite the opposite. His body felt less itchy. He could walk more freely. He stayed warm and dry.

I don't want to suggest that he emerged a fully transformed donkey, unencumbered by his old ways of seeing and being, but as he entered into relationships with us and the others in whose presence he now lived, he did work out that other ways of living were possible. Within two years of his worried arrival, whenever his feet were hurting or he had lost the others, he would stand beneath the window by the desk where I write and call out to me. Even now, when it comes to feeding time, while the others roughhouse among themselves to get to their buckets, Puzzle stands back pessimistically, makes a strange wheezing noise in my direction and follows me to the spot where I place his (own) bucket, a safe distance from the others.

L teases me mercilessly for enabling Puzzle's dysfunctional behaviour, which of course I do. We are tight. But I wasn't the only one Puzzle succeeded in recruiting into his newfound ways of managing life. Even after several other, younger and more free-wheeling donkeys arrived, Zach remained fiercely loyal to Puzzle. At the first sign of heavy rain the others would hotfoot it into the shelter, but so long as Puzzle refused to go in, Zach remained outside by his side, the two of them progressively more sodden. When Puzzle shuffled anxiously, looking sideways at the vet examining his feet, Zach would hold Puzzle's lead rope in his mouth. And when Puzzle failed to realise that the others had moved on, and inevitably got left behind, Zach would find a high point on the land, raise his head towards the sky and give out a clarion call that rang across the valley. Living with them day in day out I have heard the donkeys bray in a range of circumstances – for food, because they get stuck on the wrong side of a fence, when they are chasing each other across the field or through the copses, when they are demanding our attention. Never do any of them make the sound that Zach makes when he is calling out to Puzzle. That seemingly simple note is doing complex work: simultaneously sending a friend the encouragement he needs to snap out of the sense of hopelessness he falls into when lost and providing a sonic map to guide him to company and safety.

Anyone who has seen a donkey, or even a picture of a donkey, knows that their ears are idiosyncratically long, but their length tells you nothing about how those ears behave. Like moving antennae they turn and tilt in the direction of sounds we cannot even detect, let alone locate. To say that they provide an extraordinary capacity to hear is not the half of it. Those ears are the passage between attunement, receptivity and responsiveness. As their ears are working away to provide an acute point of contact with the world, their whole bodies respond to the changes they detect, usually in the first instance with the tension of alertness, and then, depending on how they read the sound, with swift, agile and definitive movements.

I am not suggesting that donkeys can't or don't miss changes in their environment. And even if they were sensitive to each signal and ready to respond, they might not have the capacity to make the adjustments they would need to make to survive an emerging threat. But I have been struck by the way they combine acute attunement and receptivity on the one hand and piercing clarity of communication on the other. When Zach places himself on the top of the hill, raises his head and makes his call, I have never seen the others ignore it. They seem incapable of ignoring it. If his bray call happens to come in the middle of the night I always wake, alerted with the rest of his community to the possibility of a danger to which I ought to be alive.

People who come to visit here often comment on the deep quiet. In a sense they are right. But the place is actually a symphony of sounds – the donkeys' calls and responses, Jimmy's low rumble when he hears us approaching, the sheep's *'maa'*s when one of them gets separated from the others, the birds calling out to each other or to the dawn and dusk, the river's shifting intensity with the coming and going of the rain. Sometimes, especially near the dawn, the sounds are so dense you need to raise your voice to be heard. It might seem odd, then, that what most overwhelms me when I go into the city is the noise. The assault of demands on my sensory, intellectual and emotional attention has me ricochet between numbness and hypervigilance. I know that I need to pay attention so I can judge wisely, but in the saturation of signals, most of which signify nothing but rapid movement and construction, it is difficult to discern and to attune at the same time. I find myself a little like Puzzle, choosing to keep my head down.

At the end of one of her reflective essays on the human condition, Hannah Arendt, one of the most incisive minds of the last century, described a cultivated person as 'one who knows how to choose his [sic] company, among men [sic], among things, among thoughts, in the present as well as in the past.' Constrained (as we all are) by the bounds within which she lived and thought, Arendt was unable to recognise the full range of those with whom we might keep good company. I doubt she would have imagined that the company of animals other than humans, or of plants, trees or ecosystems could also shape who one became. Still, her choice of the word *cultivation* implicitly takes us to the land. When I'd acted on the intuition that coming to live in this place would shift my shape I'd not yet realised the degree to which that work would be effected through the company I would come to keep, among all the beings, among all the sounds, among all their practices of attention.

portents

When I hear the cry of black cockatoos overhead I think I must be mistaken. People around here say that they come before the rain. For sure, no rain is coming today. A few years back my friend told me that Aboriginal people in some parts of Australia believe that black cockatoos accompany the spirits of loved ones after they have passed into the land of the dead. Ever since, they have carried the trace of death and numinosity for me. They are huge and loud and glorious, and they occupy the sky with a sense of entitlement that leaves me feeling a little deferential towards them. Not that I begrudge them that; deference seems like the appropriate attitude to hold in the presence of the ancient and the magnificent.

Even when the direction of their flight looks random to me they always seem to have a sharp sense of where they are heading.

One afternoon about three years ago L and I were sitting with a neighbour over a bowl of olives and a glass of wine when a mob of what must have been forty or fifty flew across the valley, escarpment to escarpment. We did not see them all at once – seven coming from the east, twelve coming up from over the river from the west, another twenty coming into view after a few seconds' delay – until they joined up in a loose but unmistakable formation. Their cries drowned out our conversation, but even if they hadn't, the majesty of the sight would have commanded our silence. Some birds just have a way of putting you in your place.

Occasionally when I am on the porch reading I hear the distinctive sound of a few of them giving a tree nearby an absolute trouncing with their hooked beaks. I've learned the wisdom of looking up and taking some moments to watch them and not just giving in to the jealous claim that what I call 'my work' unfailingly makes on my time. If I can make them out amidst the branches and leaves, I watch them at work digging grubs out of the bark. Their focus and determination – enlivened, I imagine, by the tastiness of success – is arresting. For a few weeks during spring, three black cockatoos occupied a grove of trees just at the top of the field where the goats and sheep live. I presumed they were a couple and a fledgling who had not yet gone out on his own. At that time of year the trees must have been fruiting with a berry they were particularly fond of. They occurred to me like phantoms, whose comings and goings lay completely beyond my control, but their temporary permanence felt like a benediction.

This morning it is just two or three, and I hear their calls as I'm making my way down to my neighbours' place. Like us, they have decided that the time has come to get all of the animals out. In that ancient past, a couple of weeks ago, when all of this was still abstract and we were extrapolating from what had come before, we'd judged that there were safe places to leave the animals to navigate their way through a fire, should it pass through their land. Even the way that we imagined fire 'passing through' exposed our failure to appreciate what was happening. Making the call now, leaves crisp under our feet, desiccated air, strings of days over 40 degrees, stories of walls of fire breaking through containment lines clattering around in our heads, those plans have come to look like death sentences. There is no passing *through* these fires. In fact, now that they are engorged by the fuel they have been consuming for weeks and incited by the winds they have helped to make, there is probably no passing *by* these fires.

In these weeks of watching, I've been closely observing how the animals have been responding. Ziggy is a small, exquisitely beautiful fawn-pink donkey who never hesitates to move right in close and check out what I am up to. As the fires moved south from the north, and north from the south, he started to shy away every time I approached. And, because I trust their knowing, because day in, day out I see evidence that they live with perceptual capacities we seem to have lost, the change in him was as frightening for me as the changes on the satellite images. In the middle of the night, a few days before we anticipated that the fire was going to reach us, lying in bed, doing what I would soon come to do in bed every night – not sleeping – I decided that the next day was the day we were going to move on getting everyone out. For a couple of weeks already, the huge fire to the south had been ebbing up to the river like a shifting tide. Sometimes it licked the riverbanks, and then a wind change would draw it back south and we could breathe out again. No one believed for a moment that game would last forever.

As soon as it breached the river it would rip through the wooded valley that hugs the northern banks and then travel north on the back of the southerly wind that whips up each afternoon, veering east or west according to its whim. Still, we had the good fortune of a few days' warning, and I was not going to wait until everyone's panic levels – including the animals – had reached fever pitch as the distance between us and the fire wall shrank.

Now, less than two days later, almost everyone has gone. I've still to work out how to get the sheep and the ducks out. The donkeys, horses and goats were all evacuated yesterday and I spent the evening settling them into their temporary homes. M arrived early this morning and we walked Jimmy and Katy up the hill from their world to her float, coaxing them with a bucket of carrots. I stood at the gate watching them recede as they drove down the hill, until they turned the corner and I could not see them anymore. It felt empty, not quiet. I felt hollow and noisy.

As I come down the hill I see that my neighbour and her daughter are loading their stuff into an old horse float on the side of the road while they wait for some people to arrive with a truck large enough to evacuate their seven horses. The same folks brought their truck to us yesterday; beneath the dirt that clung to their sweaty bodies, they looked to me like angels with none of the fanfare. I've wandered down to my neighbours today so that I can return a stock-whip the angels left leaning in one of the stables after they'd pulled it out to convince the donkeys to get into the truck. It's complicated being an angel these days.

Barely visible through the high shrubs in the paddock over the road are the two ponies, one dapple grey and one a dark chestnut, almost as wide as they are tall. They are a local fixture, often stopped in the middle of the road when you come around the bend near their home. You could get out of the car and try to coax them off the road if you liked, but they tend to take their time and move at their own pace. Sometimes, if I am heading home during the day, I get out, less to try to move them along than to hang out for a few moments before we each go on our way. The smell of horses, their breath sweet with the grasses or flowers or shrubs they've just moved on from, has never ceased to intoxicate me.

My neighbours tell me how bolstered they feel to see the black cockatoos; maybe it is going to rain and maybe the rain will dampen the fire. I'm not sure what to say. They seem to be clinging to the possibility of reprieve. I don't want to be unkind.

I duck the comment rather than make mention of the other symbolism, which is far more present to me just now.

I am not much into what I see as idle hope, but then I can hardly claim to be spotless myself; we all need to hope for something. Do I hope that it is going to rain tonight, so much, in fact, that it will douse a fire that has been raging across several thousand hectares for two months? No. Do I hope that we humans will find our way to making the changes we need to make to avoid mass extinction and the complete breakdown of civilisation? Yes.

I've developed a highly ambivalent relationship with hope these days. If I hold on to it at all, it's mostly as a strategic act – a way of orienting myself in the direction most likely to keep me in action. Perhaps there are people on this planet with the capacity to stay in action and kindness even after they have let go of all hope; I want it to be true that there are people with that type of fortitude. But for now, and for me, those two – hope that our actions might prevent at least some of the death and the loss, and my capacity to commit myself to taking those actions – are still joined at the hip. As climate justice essayist Mary Annaïse Heglar puts it, if you want to have hope, go out and earn it.

I want to be totally straight here, though. I'm not always up to reality. I have also been seduced by the type of magical-thinking hope that promises an antidote to the noxious brew of fear and helplessness that has, at times, consumed me. In early December, when a neighbour pointed out that we needed to keep an eye on the large and expanding fire to the south, not only did I hope that, by some chance, it would *stay* away, I went so far as believing that if I did not pay attention to it, it would *go* away. Not unlike the baby wombat who, over the winter and spring months, would come out with her mama in the afternoon and early evening and meander in the large paddocks where the horses like to spend most of their time. From a distance we could observe her dark round body waddling around, never too far from her mama. But if we came too close she would sneak her face in behind her mama's much larger and similarly round body. She could not see us, so obviously we could not see her. It's not a bad strategy, so long as you have a larger, wiser, more astute being nearby who will reliably jostle you into a safe dry burrow as soon as the danger actually materialises. We humans, being endlessly creative, allow fantasy to play that role.

Apart from its more tangible provocations, this summer has offered up a rich array of Petri dishes for observing how we, human animals, respond to danger – both the immediate danger of fires approaching, and the other longer-term dangers that they signify. Perhaps because we are attuned to protect our bodies and the bodies of those we care about, the people whom I have witnessed facing immediate and palpable dangers seem to respond in ways you might call 'rational'. In other words, once the danger is at their door, they take the actions most likely to produce the outcomes they desire, which seems to me like a pretty good definition of rational action. If you do not want to die, and you want to save the lives of loved ones – human and non-human – move away from the source of danger. If you, or they, cannot get away, protect yourselves in whatever way you can. I'm not underestimating the huge amount of thought, planning and sheer energy it is likely to take to do this well, and whatever you do might not work out in the end. The graph can always diverge from its predicted course when the unanticipated occurs or when the causes of disaster start to double back on themselves. Still, there is a certain simplicity to the way we respond when the dangers are, as we like to say, clear and present. When it comes to the dangers that are not at our door, that simplicity seems to dissipate. Then all sorts of strange growths start showing up in the Petri dish.

There is the techno-triumphalist response: *We will defeat whatever is coming at us through a combination of technological ingenuity and sheer human will.* There is the disdainful I've-been-there-before response: *There is nothing new or particularly daunting here, this is a sunburnt country, spare me your snivelling panic.* There is the staunch refusal response: *I do not accept that, cease wasting my time.* And then there are all of the responses that social psychologists have been documenting among us humans in the face of terrifying, existential threats since the Cold War went nuclear: distraction, doom, and fanatical faith in the strong and decisive leader (on earth or elsewhere) whose body you can hide behind and who is promising a safe, possibly even eternal, burrow.

I have smelt a bunch of them right up close over the summer and since. Wearing my heart on my sleeve as I do, those expounding their particular version of denial to me tend to do so with a good dose of condescension. As if there is something offensively effeminate and sentimental about taking seriously the prospect that we humans are hurtling towards the mass killing of ourselves and everything around us. Sometimes I have the presence and poise to try to speak as if we were having a reasoned conversation about how best to protect all of us from a future

I can't but imagine they don't also want to avoid. More often I literally bite my tongue. Occasionally I fail at both. What tends to tumble out then are carefully chosen analogies – horrors I surmise will most deeply flummox them (everything from the death of their children to a past genocide), usually laced with a good dose of fury and sarcasm. It's not a winning strategy.

Back on the side of the road, my neighbours and I share our speculations about where we think will be safest for the animals, along with anecdotes about the kindness of the strangers who have shown up to take them there. We chat about the old guy up the road who says he is going to be staying put. He's seen fires come and go. He still believes that we are safely tethered to old cycles. We exchange stories about the firefighters coming by to tell us they wouldn't be coming back. They came by to make sure they had a list of the names of everyone who lived up here, and a record of our plans: when we think we will leave, if we think we might stay.

I tell my neighbours that we will be heading out soon, most likely to stay close to the horses and donkeys towards the coast. Probably in the next few days. Same for them. We wish each other well. We don't make plans for when we might see each other again. Another neighbour had turned up at our place the previous evening to share an excellent bottle of red he had found lying around the house. Better drink it now, which we did. We drank it for the pleasure of drinking it, not to toast the future.

I wander back to the car, hop in and turn it around. When I get partway back up the hill, I stop, get out and look up to check for the black cockatoos. When I catch sight of them again, there are more – maybe ten or twelve. They are flying in a loose but connected formation, squawking in their uniquely expressive way, perhaps to each other, perhaps just towards the sky. It occurs to me that maybe I mistook their alignment and attentiveness to each other and to everything around them for a clear direction and a determination to get there. They could just be responding to their mates, to the winds, to the appearance of berries and grubs in the trees, or water on the ground, to the shifts they observe in dryness and temperature. To the spirits of loved ones passing into the land of the dead.

during

australia

It is the morning of New Year's Eve, and this is Australia.

It's only eight o'clock, but as soon as I open the door the heat of the coming day permeates my skin. I walk out the laundry door, round the side of the house and over to the concrete slab where the water tank and the gas bottles sit. I pick up the wrench and try to remember how to disconnect the gas so that I can roll the bottle out into the field. That way, if it explodes from the heat of the fire, it will be some distance from the house. Every preventative action counts.

It's not the type of work I normally do. But this morning L is long gone, driving to Sydney in the truck we packed last night with what we could not bear to lose. The paintings that became ours when my parents died. Photos of my grandparents from before the war, and of our kids when they were little. A dowry bag made by a woman in a village in Pakistan and given to us by a family who fled across the border to Jaisalmer. A few books. Residue of human creativity that we held in our custodianship, and to which we feel a responsibility. All packed into the truck between cardboard and pieces of foam we dragged over from the barn, wrapped in every sheet and blanket I could find in the cupboards. It has not been lost on us that we are among the very few who have the luxury of a few days' warning to save what is most precious. Leaving aside, of course, that you cannot take the trees, the native animals, the grass, the soil, the river and the relationships that sustain us all.

For some days now, our community has had a single focus: *Protect each other and the animals we live with from the fire*, which is ever closer. Who has horses that need to be evacuated? Who has a paddock that is safe? Who has a space cool enough for chickens not to expire in the heat? Who has a room where people who are evacuating with an old dog can come and stay? People's needs and the impulse to respond to them are spread over this land like a spiderweb. It is only three days ago that three trucks turned up at our place, less than four hours after I put out the call that I needed to get the animals out before the fire crossed the river. I had not previously met any of the people who turned up to help. We still don't really know each other's names. One man literally lifted the locked-in-terror bodies of my donkeys up a makeshift ramp onto his truck and drove them to their temporary home, where L and I would soon join them. I see my neighbours' cars and utes and troopies, boots and hatches open, as they scurry back and forth, loading them with whatever they have had time to decide is most precious to them. We have never spoken so frequently, so urgently with each other, but I've not heard a single mention of New Year's parties, resolutions, champagne. The annual New Year event and fireworks in town were cancelled when the showground was turned into an evacuation centre for animals from across the district.

With temperatures set to ascend into the 40s by around 11 am, and a fierce southerly predicted to come up in the mid-afternoon, we've all been warned that this New Year's Eve is going to be a bad one. Early morning on days like this is a dangerously deceptive time: wind still relatively calm, heat relatively mild, the icons that mark the status of each fire on the Fires Near Me app still fall within the calmer side of the colour spectrum. The people on the radio still adopt a tone of anticipation, not contained urgency. In the morning you can still tell yourself that it's not going to go the way we feared after all. We think we are creatures of reason but I have been struck of late by the degree to which thinking always first passes through our bodies. How the way we make sense of what is happening around us is shaped by the quality of the light, the intensity of the heat, the strength of the wind. Eight-thirty and the wind is already stronger than my body wants it to be.

When I come back in after rolling the tank out into the field I check my phone. It's odd that I didn't take it outside with me; we are usually fused in a deadly obsession. I touch the screen and see the box telling me I have a missed call from M. It appears immediately below my unsent message to her from last night: 'I hope everything is OK with you guys. I'm worried about the fires down there. Please let me know if you need anything.' The reception is lousy up here and that message never made it. The little red exclamation mark that signifies a failed message is still there next to it.

Already on edge, I grab the landline and call. M picks up right away.

I have to tell you how hard it is to write this. My fingers have stopped, and again I feel that sheet of metal down the front of my body. I very much want you to know that this is not a story. We are so damn used to stories, underscored by music and illustrated with images, that reality, hot or dead, has become near impossible to grasp. I am pretty sure that anyone who has received a call about a loved one being dead or seriously ill or injured knows exactly what I am talking about. I am sorry if this is traumatic for you. But if we don't find a way of breaking open this veneer of virtual reality, our encounter with reality will come too late. We have due warning.

She picks up. 'It's all gone.' She is standing in the middle of the black, she tells me.

'Jimmy and Katy?' I ask.

She tells me that the fire came from three sides and everything is destroyed. She tells me how she lay on the floor of the house and tried to catch the little oxygen that remained. She tells me that as she lay there it all went from a deafening roar to deadly quiet. Then the fire blew in the windows. She tells me that she looked up and saw the fire rush inwards from the corners to form a swirl on the ceiling, up to the crescendo that exploded the house as her partner dragged her out.

I am vaguely aware that I need to contain the eruption that is occurring inside me because I am speaking with someone standing in the midst of the devastation of her life, someone who just witnessed what she thought was her death. She tells me her horses have survived – she has no idea how – but they are burnt. I do not push the question about Jimmy and Katy. She has given me the answer.

When I hang up, the emptiness of the walls is a violent presence. The heat is nauseating. My thinking has stopped, and the information I have just heard seems to have taken on a strange type of existence – detached words, words that I can decipher but that hang for a while in some type of limbo before they gain the weight of an actual referent. But I call L with those words in my mouth, knowing full well that they are going to undo him even as he is unpacking the truck that he still needs to drive back home and then likely back again when we evacuate later in the day. But the words belong to him too. I need to give them over.

When he doesn't answer, I call our friend who met L in Sydney to help him unpack. She does pick up and I ask her to put him on. She knows from my voice not to ask. I cannot for the life of me remember the words I used to tell him. I cannot remember what we planned to do, or saying goodbye, or putting down the phone. I can remember the return to nothing after I'd hung up.

The stillness of the house – just the dogs and me – leaves too much space for M's words to bounce around the walls and into my head. When Jimmy and Katy disappeared down the road two days ago I said I felt hollow. Now it's a negative space, like a vacuum I might get pulled into. I muster whatever mental stamina I have not to succumb to a story where I am to blame. I can't afford that type of self-indulgence right now.

I call the dogs into the car and drive down to feed the donkeys and horses and clean up their paddocks. The sun is beating down and I know I should not be out there, but it needs to be done and I need to be doing. The work consumes my body and the sun beating on the back of my head absorbs my attention. And I need to be near their life. When I am done I head into town. There are emergency provisions I need so I can't avoid it, but I know it's a bad choice.

It is now around lunchtime, and there are couples and families sauntering along the street, eating gelato, buying knick-knacks. Wallaby tea towels, locally blown glass vases, carved wooden bowls. Normally tourists are a source of delight for me. Their pleasure is palpable, and their presence, and the desires they bring with them, provides sustenance for the town. But today I see them through a film of bitterness. I find myself on the other side of a new, malign fence. A man abuses me for leaving the dogs in the car while I run into the store to buy batteries for the emergency-kit torch. The words to convey that I left the car running and the air conditioning on, and that Katy and Jimmy are dead, gather in my throat. But his face is so angry, and I am feeble. I stammer something vaguely defensive and get into the car. I see him return to the table on the footpath with his friends.

The annual summertime ritual: a few days away from the city at the end of a long, time-poor year. At last there is time enough for late breakfasts and slow afternoons; to read whole novels and sit at footpath cafes with friends. A house near the beach; a walk around the quaint village. The gap between me and all of these other people feels inestimably vast and I look upon them with a mix of alienation and disdain. Odd to find myself on this side of my judgements; I've lolled around on summer holidays too.

I catch a few conversations as I walk down the street. I can tell who the locals are, even if I don't know them. They are the ones who aren't talking much – their faces are turned down, absorbed in thought, and their steps are determined. From elsewhere, snatches of memories and musings on the present. Folks are spooked by the extent of these fires, but *Australia has always been a terrible place for bushfires; they are just part of the landscape, necessary for the bush to regenerate.* I sense some anxiety, but it is sprinkled with analysis and indignation. *Radical environmentalists. A threat to the economy. It's important to stay sober, not to panic.*

Of late my anger has been wild and violent. Today it is gathering bile in my gut. I hear two blokes sitting on the porch of the pub bemoaning the 'fact' that the greenies got in the way of the controlled burning that would have prevented the fires. I catch sight of the front page of a newspaper condemning the arsonists and calling for harsh penalties. This pleasure in righteousness and capacity to attribute blame is only available to those for whom the unfolding reality still remains abstract. The words taste like metal in my mouth.

As I get close to home I see four cars half stuck out into the road near the waterhole popular with the locals. I stop, get out of the car and walk over. A few neighbours resent people coming up here to swim in our river, but usually it's fine with me that they are around. If people don't have a chance to touch this world they won't be moved to protect it. Today they seem like voyeurs at a funeral. Seven or eight people are lazing by the river. Their picnic is laid out on the ground. A couple of them are floating in the water. Others are chatting or sleeping over a book on fold-away chairs. As I survey them from the road it's like a scene in a slightly sepia movie.

Every other summer at around three in the afternoon, L and I come down to this waterhole to break our work with the cool of the water. We stand on a large rock, skin still warm from the sun, hesitating before we know our bodies will enter the cold, hop in and glide over to the other side where we sit, the sun drying our skin in about twelve seconds before we swim back over and head home. One of the dogs usually swims over with us. The other navigates her way gingerly over the rocks. In summer, the daylight lasts forever. I can count on one hand the swims we have had this summer, and still have some fingers left.

The New Year's Eve picnickers seem unaware that the cars passing by are packed so tight you cannot see in the windows. They are languid; we are frenetic. I ask them if they know what is happening up here and the older of the blokes assures me that he knows what he is doing, with a level of condescension that is just muted enough to pretend it's not there. I decide against a response. The dogs are barking in the car. It's as if I am two people: one from a remote past, who lazed by the river, and the one standing here now, who can't imagine that this was ever possible. You think change comes slowly, but you are wrong.

When L gets home I tell him I want to leave, to go to the city. We could stay where the horses and donkeys are, but tonight I need to be far away from here. He is exhausted and it is clear he does not want to get back into a vehicle, but he can read my mood. Then, as we are negotiating a decision, the sky turns dark. It's only 3.30 pm. The wrongness of this change in light makes the decision.

On the freeway heading north, ten, then twenty, and I think in the end more than forty fire trucks go past in the other direction. It is hard to make out the names of the places they hail from, normally written in large letters on the fender of each truck, but I catch a few of them and recognise them as places far to the north. L tells me that when he drove up and back this morning it was the same. Other than us and the occasional car, the fire trucks are pretty much the only vehicles on the road.

When we arrive in the city the switch feels surreal. Some of the roads are closed so that people can wander close to the edge of the harbour to watch the fireworks. Sydney becomes a spectacle on New Year's Eve. How many New Year's Eves have I been down there, among those crowds of people streaming into parks and onto piers to watch the lights explode into the sky over the water? How often have I peered over and down towards the harbour speckled with the lights from boats, and imagined people looking up from the dark of the water to a fully lit night sky? Tonight I want none of it.

L, exhausted from ten hours on the road, falls asleep beside me in a matter of moments, but at midnight I am awake, checking my phone for word on the fires, listening to the explosions that accompany the lights others have come across the world to see. I remember when my mother and her best friend used to take all of us kids to the Sydney Royal Easter Show. When it got dark, after we had seen the animals and been on the rides and eaten the greasy food, they would take us to see the fireworks. My mother never said she'd rather not go, but I know she hated them. They reminded her of the war. Her fear at what seemed like a marvel to me did not make sense to me at the time.

What is it about New Year's Eve that is so powerful for people? Perhaps it is that it draws people who normally occupy separate worlds together into what seems like shared time and space. The shift from one year to another happens for all of us simultaneously, and, momentarily, we share a common focus. But tonight the countdown to midnight, and the moment where the year turns, falls over two Australias: the Australia that is saturated with the reality of the climate catastrophe and the Australia for whom it remains abstract. Sure, the second Australia also knows that something is amiss; alarming images of the fires and tragic stories of people's losses have dominated the news. But like every other story in the feed, these ones also are displaced by the next ones. There is knowing and there is knowing.

Tonight, my rage at the second Australia is palpable. I know that if I open my mouth to speak with the guy at the petrol station or with the woman handing me food at the Thai takeaway, it will seep through my words. No one wants to be hectored.

Besides, when I step back and survey the various 'me's with some dispassion I see the extent to which I move across a spectrum of concern. There is the furious me of this time; there is the me who swam joyously in the river at 3 in the afternoon, even as oil spills were destroying habitats and lives, or floods were devastating communities somewhere else; there was the me who never offered to leave before the fireworks. To some not insignificant extent, who you are comes down to where you stand in relation to the catastrophe. Perhaps it is that they have not been touched yet. Not yet been burnt. Like pretty much every one of us who has assumed that our privileges are both deserved and eternal, they still believe they will be spared.

They won't be. We won't be. Right now it is that rage that wants to make everyone know that. This morning, when I sat on the floor in front of the bare walls, between calling L and going out to feed the donkeys and horses, I punched the floorboards and screamed. Like a three-year-old. It started off as desperation in the face of the indiscriminate destructiveness of the fire. Despair at the death of the animals I loved and the ones I did not know. Five hundred million wild animals dead already, and many more yet to die. But those were only the most superficial triggers. Beneath them were the more chronic sources: our intransigence, our stubborn resistance to recognising our fragility, our addiction to ways of living on this planet that have brought the fire and that have brought us here.

There is a reason that we have imagined hell as fire. At that moment my grief is about as infinite as my rage is murderous.

death

I told you that Katy died. But that initial telling was about the impact of her death on others. On me, standing in our half-emptied-out house when I heard M's voice over the phone. On L, perched on the back of a truck, unloading the contents of our house, when he heard my voice over the phone. And on Jimmy, who didn't have to hear about it because he was there, with Katy, until the moment he walked into a life without her.

I also did not tell you a lot about how she died, or what death might have been like for her. That was in part because I wasn't there, so my knowledge of what happened is sketchy. It was in part because, for a long time, Jimmy's loss took up all of my mental and emotional space. So long as that was the case my access to Katy's death was mediated by Jimmy's grief. And if I am honest it was in part because the zero point of a death, especially a death that involved immeasurable suffering, is difficult to approach. Now it's time to talk about Katy. Or, more precisely, about Katy's death.

When we arrived to collect Jimmy and take him home from the fire zone there were no people around – save the men up at the top of power poles and their mates down below in trucks, calling out to each other as they tried to restore the powerlines that had been melted by the fire. M and her partner were in town, filling out forms with the Red Cross. As arranged, we called ahead to let them know we were approaching, but couldn't reach them, so we continued up the driveway to the spot where it was evident that the house and garage had once stood. Torn and tangled corrugated iron. The remains of brick walls. A burnt-out barrel or two. Blackened, brittle remains of shrubs. A structure that looked like a guest cabin stood intact, with cups on the counter and a few green carry bags on the wooden floor.

Katy's body was lying on grass-become-charcoal behind a screen of blackened twigs that I guessed were the remains of what must have been the garden around the house.

I saw her from some distance before I had a chance to decide whether I wanted to see her. And then I thought about whether to look away or to take in the sight of her. I know how certain images can haunt you. Once seen they cannot be unseen. Like passages in books describing unspeakable cruelties: as soon as I had read them I'd wished I had not. Or perhaps it is more accurate to say that as soon as I'd read them, I knew they were going to be with me for good, and that this was going to have consequences. It is an ethical dilemma, whether to know or shield oneself from knowing.

There was no mistaking that this was Katy. The shape of her back is so distinctive. Only now it was charred black, with one or two patches of her once pink flesh visible through a honeycomb of burnt skin. Her back legs were sticking up in the air, and although it too was burnt I could see the pettitoe at the end of her top leg, still dainty. My daughter used to joke that it looked like Katy was walking on high heels because her pettitoe feet always looked ill-proportioned against her rotund body. I could not see her head or her face because it was rounded down away from me. From here it almost looks like she stops at her neck. I decide to go a little closer. She is, after all, Katy, and I owe it to her to see what she has become in this fire. She had no choice but to go through it. I can bear witness to what remains.

When I got closer, what I saw was that her entrails had spilled out onto the ground. It had been eight days and a few hours since she was killed. Eight days in January in south-east Australia and she had lain split open, through the unrelenting dry heat. The absence of a putrid stench struck me as odd. By now her body was parched. Perhaps the time of the stench had passed. I was relieved at not being consumed by the nausea I would no doubt have experienced, but it was also disconcerting, as if the perceptions coming in through my different senses didn't match up.

I want to be able to tell you about her face, but I cannot. Either I did not look closely or I did, but I can't recall what I saw. Most likely I stopped short just there, at her face, because looking into that face had been such an intimate privilege, from her always tentative grey eyes down to her magnificent shiny-at-the-front nose, up to the stretch of forehead, and then to her huge ears, the points bent down at the top. That she would look at me when I was looking at her was an achievement we had worked for together. Now it could only be me looking at her. Which seems to me to be the literal experience, and not merely the concept, of another's death. I touch the aloneness of the moment. Or rather, it touches me.

It is true, there is a sense in which a back or a leg or a shoulder also responds to an other's presence. It softens or tenses, inclines or retracts, comes near or moves away. But in the face-to-face encounter there is something else – a reflexive recognition that we are each, and both, regarding and responding to each other. Philosophers call it 'theory of mind': knowing that the other knows. It's like mirrors that return one another's reflection over and again. Katy and I were in no doubt that each of us knew. The challenge for me was to bring enough discipline to that encounter to quiet my own assumptions about what knowing meant, so that I might get a sense of how Katy knew. The challenge for Katy was, I am guessing, to bring enough trust to the encounter to still her desire to look or move away, so that she might get a sense of what I knew. When we managed that, what we knew oscillated between the mundane and the miraculous. That she wanted water and I could go and turn on the tap. That she felt gratitude and that I felt grace.

So, I probably could not – or would not – bring myself to look at her face when she could no longer look back at mine. I do recall her ear – that is, the one that I could see, because the other one was hidden under her head, pressed to the ground. The ear retained its perfect, unique pig's-ear shape – narrow at the bottom, then rounding out in the middle and then coming to a point – only it was black. The point was tipped slightly down, as if it had a little fold in it. And although I did not touch her ear I could tell that it was no longer soft the way it had been when she was alive, but dry, hard and brittle.

A pig's ear. I went onto a website last week to buy a few things I needed for the dogs. After I had clicked my purchases into the electronic basket, the site's artificial intelligence offered me an array of bestselling products it presumed I might also like to buy. Among the top three was a packet of pigs' ears – dried, copper-coloured and shiny – ready for your dog to chew. Their algorithms must tell them that lots of people express their love for their dogs by treating them with pigs' ears.

Just last week a friend, whose first language is not English, wrote to me, shaken, after she heard the expression, 'turning a sow's ear into a silk purse' for the first time. A sow's ear, she wrote, is what allows the sow to 'hear her world, her babies, danger approaching, food on the way'. By contrast, a silk purse derives its value entirely from humans' aesthetic pleasure in its fabric, and, aptly, its functionality in carrying the coins of our realm. It is thanks to the 'self-evidence' of their comparative value that the expression works so well as a self-executing idiom. We do violence without even thinking about it. Katy's ear is not that pig's ear.

Katy must have been close to the house when the fire came. I was told that some of these fires, at their fiercest, moved at seventy kilometres an hour, or over one kilometre every minute. In dimensions we can readily grasp, a fire at that speed will cover 120 metres in a bit more than ten seconds. An Olympic pool in four. With those ears and that nose, Katy must have heard and smelt the fire long before it became visible, but from the moment it came over the hill into her vision she would have probably had less than a minute to get away, had there been anywhere to go. Wherever Jimmy was when he found a way of surviving – in the dam or in some spot that was randomly spared – must have been where, or very near where, he happened to be when the fire materialised.

Probably Katy was near the house, near M, who had always protected her, and so she stayed there on the presumption that this was where she was most likely to be safe. Maybe she was a little way away and ran back there. Maybe she was even trying to run to where Jimmy was but didn't make it. Whatever the direction of her movement, it stopped there, where her body remained when we saw her.

That she died thus sticks in my throat as though I have swallowed a piece of gravel. You have to drag yourself through the sludge of thick resistance to make vivid for yourself the truth that someone you love died a violent and agonising death. Part of what it means to love someone else is precisely to be committed to protecting them from violence and suffering. In this finality of violent death you have to face your failure. Don't get me wrong, I'm not talking about some deluded fantasy of omnipotence. I had long ago given that up. This is a more sober acknowledgement of our inevitable finitude.

In Katy's case, that finitude carries a particular irony because we humans have our fingerprints all over the violence that pervaded her life *and* the attempt to curb it. At one end of that life, animal activists had scooped her and Jimmy up, tiny and starving, from the factory-farm floor where they had been left to die, presumably not considered worth the cost of food. It was those people's witnessing and refusing of the slow violence from which Jimmy and Katy were dying that carried those babies into their (and our) future lives. Lives that were characterised by care and protection and love. I have photos that M gave me of Jimmy and Katy in minuscule jackets she had knitted to keep them from dying from the cold – emaciated, scarred and terrified as they then were. And when M could no longer keep them she had placed them in our hands, to provide them with whatever the equivalent cover was for adult pigs in a world where pigs' ears get to be what pigs' ears signify.

In the beginning, human violence took on a form of disposability. In the end, human violence took on a form that escaped human control: the fast violence of our fire. In the end, depending on where you stood, Katy went back to be counted among the 'livestock' that was 'lost' in the fire; or she remained Katy, uncountable.

I have probably spent too much time since she died puzzling over the question of her life. What did that life mean to Katy? Did the violence that bookended it make it a bad life? Did the days she spent grazing or lying in the cool of the woods or sitting with me while I read and scratched her belly make it a good life? It is unanswerable, but I think that is because it is a bad question. A life doesn't comprise a set of units that can be evaluated according to a common metric and then put into an equation to produce a final summation. Besides, in the end it is only those left behind who have the temerity, or perhaps the confusion or the grief, to ask questions about the value or meaning of a life. Katy simply lived it. Until she died.

The philosopher Emmanuel Lévinas once wrote that suffering is useless for the ones who suffer, but perhaps not so for those who are present to another's suffering, especially if they cannot alleviate it. I slightly recoil at the notion of suffering being useful or useless, as if it is a means, effective or ineffective, to some ends. Still, encountering the reality of Katy's death has done something to my capacity to love, to the quality of my love, to the reach of my love. To the wonder I experience at life, and to my desire to protect it. And that is something else altogether.

dusk

It is the evening of 3 January. The malevolent rhythm that arranges the days is becoming familiar. One day of crisis, a few days of relative calm, one day of crisis. We have returned to the land, but it doesn't feel much like home, with the animals still billeted out to their evacuation stays, our days consumed by watching the shifting fire patterns, the car packed for another evacuation, our bodies primed to leave again. We have just driven over to feed the donkeys and the horses at their temporary home. Until this afternoon, I had been able to place my anxiety about them in brackets, assuming that they were safe where they were – pretty far from the bush, out of the predicted line of the fire, near the coast. Cleared land, plenty of human habitation all around that people will want to protect if the fire comes. The donkeys' and horses' lives would be the collateral benefit. But now, knowing that tomorrow is going to be another catastrophic day and that the fire is closer than it has ever been, I start to see the flaws in my logic. I thought there were some walls that held us safe. Now I see they were made of dominoes, and they are falling.

First domino: the animals are safe if they are on cleared land, especially if it is not surrounded by thick bush that will expose them to intense radiant heat. Wrong. At their fiercest, these fires need no bush at all. They have already shown us that they will tear right through cleared land, fuelled not by trees and scrubs but by the oxygen alone. High-performance athletes.

Second domino: you are safe if you are near the coast. Wrong. By now we have all seen the images: thousands of people pushed right down from their homes or holiday houses or caravans onto packed beaches, even into the water; the flames burning all the way down to the dunes. Some of them will eventually need to be lifted out by the Navy. So, the 'near the coast' safety valve is leaky too.

Third domino (the game only works if there are a few): you can rely on predictive maps and so far none of them say that the fire will come as far north or east as the land where we have placed the animals (other than Jim and Katy of course). Wrong and wrong. On bad days, when the fire creates pyrocumulus clouds, any predictions about its direction are trounced by its newfound autonomy.

Final, master domino: the fire is always somewhere else. An absurd conceit that a good many of us nevertheless continue to indulge. For me it went something like this. We live in rainforest, and rainforest is different from the rest of fire-prone Australia. Safe. Then, the fires are in the north, far away. Then, the fires are in the south, closer, but still sufficiently far away. Then, the wind is taking the fires to the west, not quite far enough away. Then, the river will hold the fires back. It's as if, for so long as we can, we imagine there is a protective shield. Our culture offers us a repertoire to draw on, from the biblical to the technoscientific. But in this reality, there is no protective shield. There was none over the north or the south or the west or over any of the beings who lived there. There is none over us.

This afternoon I fell into a panic when my eyes were pulled towards the huge piles of wood stacked in the middle of the field on the land right next to where the donkeys had made their temporary home.

How could I have missed them before? What if an ember flew into them from one of those fires whose glow we can see, and they went up? They looked like recently felled trees to me, perhaps still close enough to life for the sap inside them to boil from the heat of the flames, exploding the whole pile. I imagined the seven donkeys – Zach, Puzzle, Zorro, Ziggy, Platero, Gabriel and Jasper-Dapple – no more than a hundred metres from all of this unfolding. Katy is already dead: the prospect of their bodies burning is not abstract. The vets have told me about animals who, though burnt, survived for a few days until their flesh started to fall off, and only then did they die. The threat of these beings being fenced in a paddock when a fire of that ferocity breaks loose pushes me past the point where I can think straight.

The woman whose land this is tells me that her neighbour would not be at all unhappy if those piles of wood did go up in flames; it would save him getting permission to burn them himself. It is strange to remember that not so long ago many people in the bush saw burning off as a convenient way of managing their waste. They resented laws that regulated when they could and could not set a fire on their own land. Today the neighbour and I clearly have very different ideas about what we'd like to achieve here. Our host assures me that should the fire make it this far north and east we can quickly move the donkeys to a safer part of the land. Not quickly enough, is my silent answer. If there is any threat, I am already secretly plotting to get my hands on the giant sprinklers the neighbour uses to water the commercial turf he grows and put them over the donkeys and horses. He has his ideas about getting around the law; I have mine.

I'm clearly not very good at disguising my anxiety, and twenty minutes later our host walks into the paddock where L and I are cleaning up the horses' manure, the phone to her ear. She stops to tell me she has the turf-growing neighbour on the line and hands me the phone. They both want to reassure me that he has everything in hand. His reassurance doesn't work the way he intended it to, but it does become clear to me that he places a high premium on both his valuable equipment and making sure his turf does not turn into ash. There's not much of a market for black grass. For very different reasons, then, our interests converge: to prevent a fire from starting here at all. And truth be told with fires raging across the east coast of the whole country the scope for safe places is reduced. Short of a yacht at sea, or a concrete block in the middle of the city, everywhere is vulnerable. And animals other than humans don't take well to yachts or concrete blocks.

As we drive up the mountain back to our place, L and I talk about what we ought to do next – to stay home or to evacuate again. If we leave the land, I don't want to go back to Sydney. On New Year's Eve it was distance I needed, but it's too far away from everyone else. Our equines' host has made up the bed and put out a basket of food in the little granny flat, which she has set aside for us. We'd be near the horses and donkeys and sleeping right next door to the little space where Nikolai, one of the ducks, is now confined. Since we dropped him there earlier in the day, he has been sitting and looking, a little confused, at the large plastic tub intended for making wine but now half filled with water. I don't think he gets that it's supposed to stand in for his pond.

The nights before catastrophic fire days have become heightened experiments in navigating the future unknown. We call our friend who is in the Rural Fire Service to ask his advice. In the background his wife is calling to him that we should get out now. The predicted wind change is expected sometime in the middle of the night. If the fire crosses the river then it could come to us in the dark of night. There is the option of staying up and watching the weather reports or setting an alarm to check what is happening at, say, 1 am (as if I'm going to fall asleep). But we live at the top of a winding 14-kilometre road. The only way out is back down. If the road is blocked by a fire, and we are still here, we won't get past it. If the road is filled with smoke there will be no visibility to navigate the turns as the road winds down, up, and back down the mountain. And tomorrow is going to be a gruelling and long day. Better to get out now and have a slight chance of catching a little sleep.

The thought of leaving our place and knowing that we may return to charcoal fields, the dead bodies of wombats and fallen birds, the rainforest gone, takes me past my point of toleration. But then there is something strangely comforting about our being huddled together while this is unfolding in the place that is home for us all.

When we arrive home it is dusk. The light has that strange quality it has assumed since the fires started; and although going anywhere near the aesthetics of this muted sun feels obscene, sometimes you cannot but be taken by the curious beauty. L goes outside to check the water pumps that he has worked round the clock to set up, but which will end up not working. Apart from the dogs and the sheep next door, whom I tried to get out but who refused to be caught or to go into a trailer, all of the 'domestic' animals have gone, so I come inside and sit at the table to gaze out over the disappearing valley and write. A friend once told me that I had a nostalgic relationship with the past. He was half right; I also have anticipatory nostalgia. I look at them all – the ferns by the pond; the wood ducks upon it; the cherry trees that L planted for my birthday, knowing I had always wanted to live among blossoms; the birds whose outline I can still see, and also those I cannot see but know are there from their dusk calls; the wombats, the wallabies, the echidnas, the snakes, the frogs; the kookaburra on a low branch of the tree by the window, also looking out at them all. I look at them as you can only look upon what you fear you may never see again. If I never see them again I will not be the same person.

The word 'tragedy' has been dangerously overused during these fires. I say 'dangerously', because tragedy means that the terrible things that happen are brought down with the randomness of fate. The word erases responsibility. As if it were the gods who brought this upon us and not we who brought it upon ourselves and upon everyone and everything else. But there is nevertheless tragedy. It lies in the deepening of our capacity to recognise the irreplaceable preciousness of all these beings with whom we share this place, now that we balance at the brink of loss. In the intensification of our capacity to know our own love of, and attachment to, where we belong. As we realise that those attachments might be broken. Like all great tragedy, even as it lays bare our finitude and susceptibility to forces beyond our control, so too it gives us back a lucid experience of what it is that we care about. Would that this lucidity, and the resolve that it inspires, could hold across time, sustain itself through the distractions that inevitably follow and be passed among us intact in all its power. But like the exquisite light of dusk it is both ephemeral and apparent only for the ones who are there to see it.

senses

Twenty kilometres to the south is the northern edge of a fire that now, after more than a month, covers several hundred thousand hectares of land. It has reached right up to the other side of the river. Ready to jump. It no longer feels remote, nor abstract, but immediate and palpable.

Schooled as we are in mathematics and metrics, we have come to think that distance is defined by some type of 'objective' measurement: kilometres, miles, metres. But when it comes to how distance *feels*, it's not like that at all. Felt distance depends on what lies between you and what threatens you. Towns increase distance (no one wants a fire to burn through areas of dense human habitation). Bush that has no particular (or recognised) title of ownership attached to it decreases the distance. Unimpeded, fire can and will rip through swathes of 'unowned' bushland in less than a minute. And this summer, with fires everywhere, and all at the same time, only two scenarios are likely to bring anyone to try to stop an approaching fire. Either it is coming close to the edge of a human population of a certain size (and as our capacity and available resources to control the growing fireground diminishes, that threshold seems to be rising); or the fire is edging up against a containment line. Even then, if we once believed that containment lines meant assurance of safety on the other side, of late we have all been taken through a crash course in their mobility. Like so much else these days they are provisional.

When the fires were in the north, still well away (from *us*; they are always already on top of *some* living beings or other), I used to track them in a fairly generalised, light-on way. Most likely through the Fires Near Me app. I had never heard of it before, but now you would be hard-pressed to find someone who lives in the bush or knows someone who lives in the bush who does not have that little red square somewhere on their phone. As the fires multiplied and spread, the map came to be entirely covered by overlapping fire icons. Dread in your hand.

When fires started in the south, closer to our home, my means of watching them proliferated. I started to accumulate what I came to think of as my 'prosthetics of emergency'. I'm guessing that when most people think of prosthetics what probably comes to mind is an artificial leg that someone wears to replace a leg they may have lost in an accident or through disease. This new style of emergency prosthetics compensates for a different type of loss. Before this summer, most of us used our phone apps to find good coffee or to play music or to message family or friends. Now, when the alert sound goes off, it is not telling you that a new episode of your favourite podcast is available, but that there is a new fire in your watch zone, or that the status of an existing fire has changed. Looking back I see what a loss of assumed privilege that was, but then this is the nature of privilege: it is only when you no longer have something that you realise you were taking its presence for granted. These days when I hear a notification, my body is instantly saturated with fear. The images of fires that have proliferated across the media might begin to convey, even to those who have not seen them, something of the terror that people feel in their presence, although of course the blistering heat and the thunderous sound have been stripped away. But the notification sounds are something else altogether. They are an auditory index of my now relentless anxiety. I live either in the time before a notification or in the moments between the notification sounding, grabbing the phone and seeing what it signifies, or in the time after I have found out. You start to understand the insidiousness of the loss.

As the fires grew in number, expanded in range and approached in proximity, so too my list of emergency prosthetics multiplied till it included: a website comprising a map with regularly updated satellite images of the fires, each coded with a colour sliding across the yellow-to-red spectrum, each signalling how long ago the fire had been live at that location; both the Bureau of Meteorology (BoM) website and the BoM Twitter feed for temperatures and wind speeds and directions (doubling up in case one was more up-to-date and to manage my anxiety); Twitter for updates from the RFS (just in case they beat the updates on the app); local radio; two different Facebook groups, one for my immediate community and one for the community further down the valley, where we anticipated the fire would come from; a telephone tree; and a handful of prized contacts who were themselves in, or had mates in, the RFS.

Someone told L about an app that lets you hack in and listen to the real-time conversations taking place among the people in the fire trucks and central control. I declined that one. Like almost everyone, I need to hold on to the belief that someone is calm and in control.

So, there I was, hooked up, not unlike a patient in intensive care. But of course we (humans) are not the only ones here who have a vital interest in knowing when danger is approaching. I became very interested in what others knew, how they knew, and – a question harder to ask – what they could possibly do with that knowledge under these conditions. There is a lot of folk science around about animals picking up signals that tell them that 'natural disasters' such as earthquakes are going to happen, presumably because those types of sensory capacities increase their ability to adapt and survive. But what about *unnatural* disasters? What about fires that burn with *this* intensity, at *this* speed and over *these* types of vast areas? What happens with fires that are the outcome of the uniquely deadly cocktail of 2019: land this dry, temperatures this high and winds this fierce and unpredictable? What can animals know about the world *now*, and what options do they have to act wisely on the basis of that knowledge?

Lizards, bats and small marsupials will smell smoke and start responding well before a fire has appeared. Some beetles are so sensitive to chemicals associated with fires that they can pick them up when they are more than a hundred kilometres away. Other ground animals and birds will notice the smell or the sound of fire, or the change in temperature on different scales. All of this implies that these capacities for pre-emptive perception give them more time to do what they need to do to save themselves. But this summer we have seen what happened to koalas who tried to scoot up a tree to the high canopy to protect themselves from the fire that was burning the tree's trunk and lower branches. That survival strategy worked for the world they had adapted to, but when flames reach up to seventy metres and the smoke plumes rise somewhere between fifteen and nineteen kilometres, no branch, however high, can protect them from incineration. In East Gippsland in Victoria, the beaches were strewn with dead birds who had tried to escape the fire by flying out over the ocean. They died from smoke inhalation or exhaustion, or both. Yellow-tailed black cockatoos, rainbow lorikeets, rosellas, parrots, honeyeaters.

As the realities of climate change receive more general acknowledgement, the idea that we need to adapt is gaining traction. Perhaps we humans will be able to accelerate the rate of technological innovation in time to develop tools that will more efficiently alert us to impending risks and afford the privileged among us some (even small) protection from these new unnatural disasters. Perhaps some people will be able to build their houses differently, change the way they grow food, even move to parts of the planet where the effects will not be so dire as to make them uninhabitable. Again, those options will be highly unevenly distributed. They already are. For all the others – all the other-than-humans, that is – adaptation will likely not be an option. They don't have the capacity to alter their adaptation rates with the rapidity required; and even if they did, they don't have access to the types of technological and material resources they would then need to build the worlds that might keep them safe. While we develop new apps and enact new building codes, others will keep climbing and dying on higher and higher branches. Or they would but for the fact that those branches might well belong to trees who cannot survive in environments remade as temperatures soar around, beneath and inside them, and their sources of sustenance evaporate.

On the morning we had decided to take everyone off the land, I went out early to call the donkeys and horses up to the top paddocks where we could easily coax them onto trucks and floats. Ziggy, that small fawn-pink donkey who had already known for days that something was awry, and his six co-conspirators were nowhere to be found. My search eventually took me to the bottom pasture: literally as far away from me as they could go. Had they been able to make their way down the narrow trail to the river, I am sure they would have been there. After months of no rain they hadn't visited the lower pasture for weeks as there was not much to eat. Besides, in this heat it was too much trouble to get all the way down there and then back to where the water was. But that morning, when I drove down in our little all-terrain vehicle, there they were, looking decidedly like they knew they shouldn't be. I called them, relying on their association between my calls and the good things that usually follow – ear scratches or food. Not so easily fooled. Even when I tried the fail-safe strategy, a bucket of the sweet-smelling food I reserve for our old horse, they would have none of it.

Did they sense my anxiety? Or did they know that there was something threatening in the larger environment? I'd been told not to try to get donkeys onto a truck once they sensed a fire nearby because they would no longer trust anyone save themselves to know how best to navigate the danger. Whatever their medium of perception was – indirectly, through my jagged emotions, or directly, to some shifts in the atmosphere – they knew that they needed to monitor the situation and be ready to take action. No yellow icon required.

As I watched their bodies respond, it struck me how thoroughly we had screwed them all. In the abstract, those who had not been domesticated might seem to have the advantage of undamaged capacities to pick up shifts in wind and heat, and to notice the responses of others around them – insects and birds who were even more attuned to changes in the earth. Unconstrained by us they would, hypothetically, be able to act on what their attunement told them. But in the face of *these* fires, even the most astute, strategic and fast animal would have little chance of survival. And besides, already pushed into fractions of a habitat crisscrossed by roads, they are never truly unconstrained by us.

As for the ones who had been domesticated, perhaps they retained some of those capacities, but the photos of dead burnt animals caught on fences as they were trying to escape is testament to the malevolence of their imprisonment. And it is not just the single immediate act of confinement that has undermined their capacity to survive. It is the centuries or millennia during which we have brought them into our world, changed their bodies, and disconnected the circuits that connect perception and repertories of action passed down generations. What did I do? I forced them onto a truck against their will. The ideal I'd sworn to only a few months ago – respecting their autonomy – looks very different this summer. Time to rethink freedom.

Since the animals have been evacuated, twice each day I have driven out from our valley, past the town and out along the straight road towards the coast where they are. It says something of my state of mind that not once have I driven the extra kilometre and a half that would take me to the ocean. I've not immersed myself in the blue cold, nor felt the waves crashing against my body, nor tasted the salt, all of which would no doubt remove me from this hot, dry, ill-lit world. But I'm gripped. I cannot detach myself.

Some days I stop along the way, pull the car to the side of the road, step out and watch the huge smoke clouds that are gathering in the distance. In their enormity, their colour and their meaning, they are unlike any clouds I have seen before. The light has been a dirty red for weeks and the smell of smoke has become so ubiquitous that I barely even notice it anymore. On some days, looking over the curves of the land to the south, I can see the red glow of the fires.

L and I are in the little granny flat, the dogs by the bed. Nikolai is in the little stall next door, but far less despondent since the arrival of his mate Fyodor, whom we brought over today from his temporary home in a friend's back garden in town. The donkeys and horses are out taking what shade they can find in their yards. It is mid-afternoon, over 40 degrees outside, and we are exhausted to the point of folding. Moments after saying that we really ought to lie down for twenty minutes, L has drifted into sleep. I am in that state of wired-tired that has become habitual. Less than five minutes after I settle down, the notification sound on my phone goes off. Either a new fire in my watch zone or the status of a fire has changed.

If you are between Town N and Town K on the west side of the highway, take shelter from the heat of the fire. Town N is about twenty kilometres south of us. I have no idea where K is. Is it north of N, in which case we are smack bang there? Is it south of N, in which case we are still okay? I'm scurrying into Google but my fingers are struggling to press the right keys on my phone. As I'm looking, a notification goes off on L's phone. I reach over his still sleeping body and grab it. *If you are between Town N and Town B on the west side of the Highway, take shelter from the heat of the fire.* We are just outside B but on the east side of the highway. In the meantime Google has come through on my phone. K is south of N. Technically that means we are safe, but at this point, the acute sense of east and west, north and south that I've acquired these weeks is as scrambled as my guts.

There is only one orientation I am attuned to and that is the one coming from the voice screaming inside my head. The acute danger that has crouched at the door for weeks is here.

I go outside. It is hot and it is windy and the sky is dead dark. I look over the paddocks to where the horses and donkeys stand rigid. They are looking south-east then south-west, necks taut, noses up. They run and then they stop and then they run again. There is terror in their bodies, and it is passing into my body. Their knowing becomes my knowing. All of the frustrations I have expressed about the vast chasm of communication that seems to separate us humans from other animals are quelled in this moment when we are standing, and sensing, here together.

after

injury

Six days since he arrived home and stopped. Since then Jimmy has remained where he is, in his world of nests that he builds himself to hold his trauma.

He was the first to come home. M said he needed to come home, and she was right. I don't know that he would have survived had he stayed on that charred ground. And Katy is still lying where we saw her. She is some way down the queue of all the animals who need to be buried. In mass graves.

I've felt deeply conflicted about having him here. I can't imagine how he could be anywhere else than in the world he knows and where he feels safe. But it is not safe. So we are here, not safe, together. Only for us it's just a matter of getting in the car and we can be gone. Not so for Jim. When we first brought him home we left the float parked with the ramp down and the back tight up against his gate, hoping we might find a way of making it an attractive house for him. That way, should we find ourselves in clear danger, I would be able to quickly coax him in. We filled it with soft straw and toys and I tried putting his food and water in there. No way he is getting back in. Not with mangoes, not with bananas, not with sweet biscuits. So I concocted a plan where, should it come to that, I would sedate him and call on enough people to place him on a blanket and lift him onto the back of the truck so we could drive him to safety. The option of leaving him is not an option.

Now most of the others are also back, and things seem to be looking up a little. The slight upswing in his mood that followed their homecoming had us wonder if, when he returned to the land still bereft of all the other animals to whom he was accustomed (save us humans), he perhaps thought that not only Katy, but everyone was dead. In the evening, he spends a little time in the field where the sheep and goats live, but generally they keep their distance from him. Remember, he is very big. And he from them. Remember, he is very alone.

Like over-protective parents who do not know how to soothe their ailing child, we have poured ourselves into cooking for him – pumpkin soup, barley broth, mashed potatoes, mango blended with bananas and papayas. Of course, he is not a child. He is another adult, but one who needs the type of tenderness that in our society tends to be reserved for children. Sometimes he likes what we make, and then not. Two nights ago, after he had refused everything, I thought to give him some leftover soba noodles. He gulped them down; but the next day his interest waned. Often he does not eat at all. He continues to lie for hours in the slightly hollowed patches of soft ground he has constructed for himself at various places in the cool of the woods. We go and sit with him, but there are times when he seems to want to be alone. He gets up with a start, takes himself to another of his nests and lies down, face away from us.

People are asking me if I think his injuries are physical or psychological. I wonder how I would make this distinction. When I am with him, feeling the lethargy in his body and seeing the absence in his eyes, what I sense is that the trauma of his mind and heart cannot be separated from the trauma in his body. The fire surrounded and entered him, taking him all of a piece.

As we navigate our determination to afford him the best care possible, we confront a background condition: pigs are not the types of beings we are set up to care for. There are few tested medications for them, save to grow them quicker. Vets don't have the facilities to treat them. For the most part we kill them when they are around six months old because after that the net profit (the sale of their body minus the cost of feeding them) starts to diminish. So we don't know that much about how to help them as they age. Luckily for Jimmy and for us a couple of vet friends who came down this way to assist with the wildlife rescues offered to see him. When they follow me, in the early morning, to check on him, he is already down in the cool at the bottom of the hill, lying in the earth. I go down alone so that he is not overwhelmed by strangers. When he hears new voices he makes his way, painfully slowly, up the hill and wanders over to greet them, hesitatingly. It is unsettling to see him so timid. We manage to peer into his mouth so we can check for ulcers from the heat. They gingerly feel his belly. They see him struggling to pee. This has been worrying me, his inability – what irony – to pass water. He has dried up.

Meanwhile, the animal sanctuary hive has kicked in and we have advice flowing in on how to keep him drinking, types of food he might like, medications that could support him and how to administer them without trauma. In the absence of a textbook course of action on how to support a traumatised pig, Jimmy's medicinal diet now comprises a pharmacopoeia of herbs and supplements, most of which I need to administer in a large syringe that I stick in the side of his mouth when – and if – he opens it to eat. It irks me to add to his unease by poking him and sticking strange-smelling liquids down his throat; but as I said, my old rules about autonomy no longer apply. He and I alike are dependent on the wisdom and care of others.

Almost every day, L and I ask ourselves whether we ought to bring another pig into his world so that he has a friend. Katy is irreplaceable, but I cannot imagine what it must be like to be alone when life has been spent side by side with another. At night, when we are lying in bed, I know that L and I are both thinking about Jimmy in his house. In the morning when we look in, there is only one indentation in the straw. For the moment he is too deep inside himself to accommodate anyone else.

We want him to be better. The people who have learned about what happened to him want him to be better. I am watching my own struggle with his drawn-out grief, with symptoms I can neither understand nor heal. It occurs to me that this experience of incompletion, of slow patience, of impotence, and of the humility forced upon me in the face of that impotence, may be part of what I now have to learn to sustain. I'm as attached as the next person is to 'things getting better', to a solution that makes this now breaking world whole again.

But when I walk back up the hill from where I find him, day in, day out, still *not* getting better, I cannot help but confront the possibility that this is not to be. Will it be possible to find peace, or some new sense of what wholeness means, in a world where brokenness and injury are not an interruption, but our condition?

ghosts

Everyone is finally home. I can resume my practice of spending a few hours every day out in the fields, hanging out with the dogs, yelling at them not to chase the wombats, watching the birds and the changing light. I return to my daily ritual of picking up the horses' and donkeys' manure and placing it in a large pile near the old blue shed, which L will turn into compost to put back into the land. There has been rain, more than we have seen in months, which is why it felt safe (enough) to bring everyone home again. Their presence makes me feel somewhat more complete, or perhaps it would be more honest to say that being able to see them here every day affords me a source of joy that creates a counterweight to the darkness that now generally envelops my perspective on the world. We are already sketching evacuation options for next summer.

The place is outrageously green. L and I are struck by the intensity of the colour, especially after the endless kilometres of black and brown that we saw when we drove south to bring Jimmy home. I say it's because of the rain. L says it's because those damned horses and donkeys have not been around to wreck his grass and his beautifully composted soil. Either way it seems impossible that we are coming back to a place that is emanating such aliveness. The donkeys and horses could not be more delighted after their exile to small rectangular paddocks where they considered what grew on the ground a poor excuse for food. When the horses arrived and walked off the back of the float they looked a little dazed and then wandered away, heads immediately down into the thick green grass. When the donkeys walked off the truck they kicked their heels into the air and hot-tailed it down to the lower pastures, momentarily glancing back at me with a look of triumph. Donkeys are like that.

Most people probably think that collecting equine manure lies somewhere between disgusting and dead boring. In my experience they could not be more wrong. It takes you right down close to the earth and close to them. And it takes you into the movement of becoming – grass, their bodies, the earth, the vegetables we grow, our bodies. Collecting the manure they leave behind means tracing where they have moved, where they have stopped, the trees that gave them shelter when they rested during the night. But for the temporal lag it places me right with them. And they sometimes hang around while I am working, or not too far away. If they don't have anything better to do they might even come up and rub against me, or indulge my penchant for putting my face against their muzzles. Since I was the ringleader in bullying them onto a truck that took them away they are a bit more cautious, but between their unremitting curiosity, their fear of missing out on what might be happening, and their forgivingness, their caution is quickly losing ground. The harms that humans do to other animals can cause permanent marks, but the animals I have known have an uncanny ability to read intention. They can discern the difference between mistakes, necessary discomforts, and malevolence.

In my fire-ravaged psyche the donkeys have come to occupy a distinctive place. They seem to be the only beings around who have not been scarred, whose sense of their place in the world has not been shaken. They still assume that it is all here for their enjoyment. They are just as cheeky and entitled as they ever were. Perfect. Let them innocently retain a way of being in the world that the rest of us seem to have lost. Let them be the placeholders for something I need to believe still exists.

As I walk around the land, I begin to see black leaves on the grass. I pick one up and see that it is a burnt leaf that has blown in. These blackened ones do not lie densely on the ground, but are scattered randomly. I take a photo of one. Appalled as I am at aestheticising suffering, I cannot deny that there is something beautiful about the black against the green. And gum leaves have a uniquely exquisite shape. In my younger years I used to screen-print them onto sheets so that we could sleep beneath them – or at least their echo.

Where did they blow in from? What happened to the tree they grew from? What about the birds that lived in or around the tree, the animals that burrowed under it, that took its shade, the mycelium with which it was in a symbiotic relationship? Is the forest in which it grew still there, debilitated, but waiting for rain to rejuvenate it? Or is it like one of the forests we saw down south: vaporised, nothing but black stumps at a distance from each other on a bed of bile-coloured ash.

Most likely it is from the forest in the south-western part of the valley out near the dam. When the fire finally crossed the river on 4 January after about two weeks of panicked expectation, it was not only electrified by an air temperature of over 40 degrees but also driven on the back of a 90-kilometre-per-hour southerly. The forests around the dam and the homes of all of the animals that live there, including the human animals, did not stand a chance. This was the type of fire that makes madness of 'stay and defend' – which, of course, is only an option for humans, who alone can acquire and master the massive technological prostheses that are needed before contemplating trying to protect yourself. Wallabies, echidnas, wombats, lyrebirds, bush rats, king parrots and all the others only have the option of stay and die. A particularly stark asymmetry when you think about who caused the fires.

Animals have always been my thing. I never had to read ethology or study animal ethics to feel our communion. I was one of those kids who preferred to be under the table with the dog than at the table with the humans. As a horse-mad adolescent I'd go to the stables before dawn and climb into the stalls while the horses were still asleep, placing my body against theirs to feel their slow warm breath. In my early twenties, when I took off from university and went to live in a shack at the back of a rainforest, I'd lean my body almost fully out of the window and try to speak to the bats as they took their evening journey. I used to joke that I was doing a PhD in bat communication. Who knew how spot-on I was about the questions that would come to most intrigue and move me?

I appreciated trees, but mainly aesthetically or as a source of peace when I was bouncing around the walls of my own psyche. I had a sense of their aliveness, for sure, but I did not experience them as co-inhabitants, as beings sharing worlds with others. Then one day, when I was being interviewed on the radio about animals and ethics, the interviewer asked me about plants. 'Doesn't your position on animals also require that we stop eating plants, given that they too might be sentient?'

I got stuck into him about posing what seemed like a disingenuous slippery-slope argument, designed to avoid confronting the stark facts about industrial animal agriculture. I reminded him that at our current rate we are killing about 70 billion land farm animals a year, of whom more than two thirds are raised and killed in industrial agriculture – a figure that rises to

99 per cent in the United States. That, even before we come to the matter and manner of their deaths, billions of animals spend their entire lives inside feed-lots, never stepping into anything resembling a natural environment, never being allowed to move freely or to form relationships. Little wonder so many of us avoid contemplating those realities and what they might demand of us. What seemed like the interviewer's desire to avoid this reality by making a point about logical consistency struck me as an example of what is most offensive about the work of the intellectual. I'm prone to anger when it seems to me that people blithely step over torture to score an intellectual goal.

But in the days after, once my anger had subsided, I reflected on his question. What about trees? If my basic stance is that living beings merit our ethical regard irrespective of how like us they seem to be, by what right do I draw a line between animals and trees? If I believe that rejecting human dominion also means refusing the idea that *we* are the ones who draw up the true hierarchy of life and then organise the world accordingly, does that not, at the very least, demand some critical reflection on the hierarchies I take for granted? The question does not mean we have to give up the idea that there are differences between different types of beings. It was more a matter of my recognising that, perhaps, at this point in human and world history, we ought to be assuming a demeanour of humility. The past assumptions that humans have made about who (human and other-than-human) ought to count don't leave a particularly enviable track record.

Even more problematically, once you realise what an absurdity the idea of the autonomous, self-sufficient individual is – be that an individual human, animal or tree – the idea that some specific types of being merit ethical respect and protection ceases to make sense. Just go out into a rainforest and take a look at the way everything is tangled up with everything else. We humans cannot see underground, but if we could we would see the network of mycelium and tree roots stretching for kilometres – not as separate beings but as one multidimensional being. Even our own bodies, which we wear with such ownership and pride and defend with such righteousness, turn out to be the product of a symbiotic relationship between the microbiome and 'us'. We rest on the earth. We eat of the sun. We breathe of the plants. We are enlivened by the rivers and the oceans. We depend on each other. We delight in all of it.

Once I started to go down this path, what really struck me was the generosity of trees. Go stand under some trees on an Australian summer day and feel how your breathing changes. Most mornings L and I do yoga in front a magnificent liquidambar tree, and when I am in tree pose (balancing only thanks to her stillness) I can stop long enough to see the home she provides, the light she filters, the *patience* she has – patience which, ever since Aristotle, we've called immobility and decided is the character of those we designate as a lower form of life. All over the world there are now schools and centres and whole sections in bookshops teaching people how to contain their movement into a type of living stillness. Tree beings contain their movement as a matter of course.

During these months, that stillness was their downfall. No evacuation. No truck to load them onto and take them somewhere safe. They live where they live, and they die where they live. The black leaves that remain as witnesses have come to rest in the fields, and they will rot there and become part of the humus that will grow other plant beings if this land does not continue to burn. There is no way of our knowing the worlds to which those leaves belonged before they were burnt off. Those stories cannot be told because there is no one to tell them. Although, right before our senses, that story is unfolding, if we are capable of reading it.

numbers

This morning, ABC Radio is broadcasting from Bega, on the South Coast of New South Wales. As with so many towns that were once names on a map, Bega now resonates with all the times I heard a radio announcer include it in a fire update. *Monitor conditions, as they may change. A fire is approaching. If you are planning to stay, start taking action now to protect yourself and your family. It's too late to leave. Take shelter in a solid structure and protect yourself from the heat of the fire.* Bega is also just a little south of Town C, where Jimmy and Katy were on the day the fire hit.

In the weeks after the fires, the fascination is intense. In Australia and across the world, the media is saturated with images of the inferno and its aftermath, with discussions of the scale and nature of the devastation and with analyses of what it all means. As distinct from other 'disasters', our collective attempts to 'deal with' what happened are not taking place in the shadow of an event that, while terrible, and even lingering in its effects, is essentially in the past. This time we prod and probe and try to find a place to steady ourselves, cowed before the spectre of climate catastrophes that loom over our future. The fire is less an event than a condition.

Two people are being interviewed on the radio. One is a woman who has spent her life providing sanctuary to wild animals just near Town C. Before the fires, the animals to whom she had offered sanctuary included 800 eastern grey kangaroos. When she returned to her home after the fire she found twenty still alive. Of the 800, for whom there was no shelter to take when the fire approached, 780 were burnt alive, died from smoke inhalation, or perished soon after from burns and injuries. We can all do the maths, but I'm not willing to risk relegating their fate to an implicit act of subtraction.

Lung damage subsequently killed two of the twenty who had held out until her return. We usually imagine that when fires of this ferocity visit an area, they burn every square centimetre, but in fact, as I saw when we went to collect Jimmy from M's place, when you walk through what was the fireground, amid the black and charred you can see random patches where the fire did not burn. If this image suggests protection, that is a visual illusion. Lacking solid structures to retreat to, wet woollen blankets to place over their bodies, and masks to cover their noses and mouths, any ostensibly lucky animals who happened upon a spared patch found themselves trapped in the midst of hot, thick smoke. Smoke that came with the fire and lasted for hours if not days after the fire's immediate presence. The woman on the radio names one of the surviving and then dying grey kangaroos: Gracy. Little Gracy stayed alive long enough for the sanctuary woman to see her die. Gracy. Grace. Blessed. Not cursed.

The other person on the program is a man who ran a sanctuary on Kangaroo Island in South Australia. Just shy of half the area of the entire island – 210,000 hectares – was incinerated by the fire. This bloke can't share figures of death or survival because he has not yet been able to return to the fireground where the sanctuary is located. It is still too dangerous. I can hear the anguish in his voice at not knowing, not being able to bring his care to those who remain alive. I mean care in the double sense: the care that might allow those for whom life is still possible to survive, and the care to ease those for whom life can only remain unbearable into an easier death. When I called our local vet just after the fires had torn through our area to connect him with the volunteer vets and vet nurses from Vets Without Borders who were on call to turn up anywhere and help, he said there was nothing for them to do. The fire had killed everyone, either immediately or in the days right after.

An unfathomable number of wild animals have been killed. Based on what we know about how many animals live in a given area of bushland and the area the fire destroyed, the current estimate is 3 billion. I am sure that number has been useful in provoking a certain intensity of shock. But I am cautious of numbers so large we cannot imagine them. Besides, numbers are flattening, as if there exists 3 billion units of some item that designates wild animals. A closer way of knowing all this death would be to bring the attention of one's mind to *this* being, who had *this* form of life and *these* relationships until they were killed. Then pause. Then move your mind to *this* being who had *their* form of life and *their* relationships, and then was killed. And then pause, and move your mind again – 3 billion times. I've done a quick calculation. If you spent just ten seconds on each of those animals, barely enough to register them as individual beings, the process would take about 950 years. Eleven good human lifetimes doing nothing but contemplating the death of animals by *this* fire in *this* country *this* summertime.

Beyond the immediacy of what happened to us and those around us I also have been permeated with the losses that have spread over this land and eke into the future. And now that the immediate danger has passed, by the realities of the period of time we mislabel 'recovery'. As I listen to these two people speaking on the radio this morning I am even more struck down than I am normally. There is something about animals being killed in a sanctuary that makes it even worse. They were there in the first place because they were the survivors of the slow violence we persistently inflicted on them: the destruction of their habitats through the seemingly limitless expansion of the infrastructure we demand to support the lives we believe we are entitled to; our careening from place to place in 2000 kilograms of metal across the paths they need to take to reach water or food; shooting them for sport; shooting or poisoning them because they compete for food with the animals we are growing to feed ourselves; draining water from the rivers that nourish their habitats and where they quench their thirst. The few who survived these myriad varieties of slow violence found protection – safety – on a few cut-out bits of land we left for them. Then there was our fast violence: the violence of the fire. Sanctuary over. It is difficult, but perhaps we ought to at least try to imagine the anguish that those few of us who have dedicated their lives to creating sanctuary are now experiencing. Connecting with their first-person experiences might take us one step closer to the animals whose anguish may be, for many of us humans, too far a stretch, schooled as we are in the arts of human exceptionalism.

Now the woman conducting the interview is speaking about the enormous grief that people in the cities are feeling about all of this death. 'Can you give them some reason to hope?' she asks. She is a fine journalist. I love to listen to her. But this enrages me. I've read the social scientific studies on the positive role that hope plays in healing and resilience. But I remain suspicious of the word 'hope' in the mouth of a culture that assumes that progress and improvement ought to be, and will be, both endless and guaranteed.

It is not that I advocate hopelessness, which has its own action-leaching pathologies. So long as we insist that hope is a dimension of action and not a feeling about the world we are passively contemplating, I'm willing to embrace it. But too often this word, this *feeling*, especially delivered over the radio, strikes me as a low-cost soporific. Placation. Immunity from the ongoing assault. A way of delivering those of us who remained safe from the direct violence of the fire a second safety from the violence of grief and the infinity of loss. It is an essential ingredient in the plotline of every popular movie. Conflict – loss or violence, accompanied by intense grief or fear; an uncertain future until a path opens up; tension over which of the paths we will choose; the right choice taken in the nick of time; closure. If I were making the movie about this summer I would insist that we stop shooting at the point of an uncertain future. At best, at the point of tension over which path to take. Even the animals who survived our fires are now dying as they search, futilely, for food that has also been incinerated by our fires. The movie would probably not get funded. Who would want to watch it?

It is not as if I am immune to finding ways of staving off the infinity of grief. There is a point at which one's body cannot hold it anymore. Your body, or my body. How is it that anyone is walking around? I remember asking myself that question in the days after my mama died (as it happens six years ago today, also my birthday). I had an answer that made sense then. That was *my* personal grief and loss. Everyone else could keep chatting on the bus or arguing with their partner or working out what to have for lunch because they had not just lost the being who had been the ground of their own being. But now the being that is the ground of *all* of our beings has been scorched and her prognosis is at best uncertain.

How well immunised we humans are. Combined, our technology and the stories we tell about ourselves make for astonishingly resilient armour. But even that armour is showing its fault lines. The suspicion that there is no mathematical rule that halts species extinction just short of humans is creeping up on us. The conviction that we have the capacity to take shelter as the fire is approaching is flagging. The knowledge that the sanctuary of human exceptionalism has no permanent immunity is seeping in.

the face

I can't quite remember all the details. That is one of the losses: the disintegration of memories of someone you love that happens in the months and years after they are gone. As I recall it, Katy came and bumped up against my leg with her huge face as I was pottering around in her and Jimmy's run. As was so often the case, it took me a while to snap out of my absorption in whatever I was ruminating on and understand that she had something very specific to tell me. She was persistent and eventually I got it. They had tipped over their water. She was thirsty. I put down the bucket, walked out the gate, made my way through the tennis-court-turned-garden, over to the tap at the end of the hose, and turned it on.

While the water was running, I came back into their area and crouched on one side of their large green plastic trough, Katy on the other side, water rising in the space between us. When she put her mouth in the cool water and began to drink she looked right at me. Amid so many shared moments this one stands out. In the two or so years we had lived together, Katy had never looked me right in the face. She would stand, facing the same direction as I was, but about half a metre in front of me, her nose pointing forward, one eye turned back and looking at me; sidelong, I think they call it. That morning, however, her eyes were on mine, face to face, as she drew the cool water into her body, the water she had so desired but needed me to fetch. I said the word 'water' – my human way of marking this sequence of our responding to each other. She looked at me and drank.

Most philosophers in the Western tradition who have thought about ethics have argued that if we are to act ethically, first we need to identify a set of principles that define 'right conduct'. For Emmanuel Lévinas, our sense of being ethically obliged is much more concrete and immediate. Perhaps this is because his work on ethics and our responsibility to attend to others' suffering emerged from his own experience as a Lithuanian Jew whose entire family was murdered in the Shoah.

His starting point was a simple observation about what life is like for most of us most of the time. We each move through our own lives and concerns, regarding everyone and everything else as part of *our* world; people or animals or environments show up as meaningful, useful, useless, interesting and so on, depending on what I find meaningful, useful, useless, interesting and so on. Then, in the midst of being absorbed in a world that is *my* world, I encounter the *face* of another person, and the world as I had experienced it, *my* world, consumed by what I wanted and what I was up to, breaks open. Another person's face stops me short. Why? Because a face can never be just an object in *my* world. The face is the site of another's experience, never reducible to what I know or what I want. The other, like me, is looking out at her world. How the world occurs to her, from her perspective, always exceeds and is different to how the world occurs for me. Again and again, and in each case otherwise, the face makes it impossible for me to turn *the* world into *my* world. This, he writes, is the beginning of ethics.

When I first read Lévinas I thought I had come across the most important idea in the world. And I thought I had found in him a thinker who invoked the world I wanted to be part of. But Lévinas insisted that only humans have faces. Only humans have this infinite and irreducible view out onto the world. And what followed from this was that only humans are capable of calling other humans to this place we call ethical responsibility. Only when we are face to face, human to human, can we say not simply 'I want you', but 'I want you to have the life you want. I want you to be'.

But then there is Katy's face over the water. And I wanted her to be. And when I saw Katy's charred body lying near the flattened ruins of the house where she had run when the fire came, I wanted her to be. I wanted to find myself face to face with her once more. More than that, even if I could never see her again, I wanted her to have a view out onto her world.

And it is not just Katy, or Katy's kind, or even animalkind. Lately, after the long dry months, the huge fronds of the tree ferns that live all around us have changed from an almost iridescent green to burnt brown. Not fire-burnt, but from the slow scorch of unrelenting sun and the lack of water from the inside. The slow violence of drought. We thought they were dying but one of our neighbours who knows plants well explained that they had pulled the water back from their fronds and into their trunks so they could weather out the dry. When the rain finally came, it was as if they started to let themselves exhale a little, hints of green coming back into the fronds. Still mainly brown, because it was too early to trust that the rain would continue, but not quite so wary in their contraction. I have an inkling of their faces.

I am trying not to anthropomorphise here, but it is hard not to, because humans – at least humans who speak my language – have taken all the best words and guarded them jealously for ourselves; all the words that signify feeling, wanting, knowing, responding, aspiring. At best, everyone else gets to react. So, as long as I'm using this language, there really is no option than to use the words that we humans apply to ourselves and claim as our human affordances and capacities, but use them in the spirit of resistance. To trust that when we give them over to beings other than humans – to Katy or to the ferns, or to the ecosystems that are trying to persist as temperatures soar and water stops – those words will also have the chance to change, to lose their selfishness. And perhaps they will even have something to offer us in turn. Who knows what we might be like if we shared those capacities and the chance to define them with others?

It is not that there are no other ways of being human, nor other ways of knowing and speaking. In recent years Indigenous writers and friends have given me the opportunity to peek into worlds where humans live among other beings with an appreciation that they are also making sense of their worlds. These human worlds are teeming with diverse, related and knowing subjects across the spectrum of being and well beyond the human. As Robin Wall Kimmerer, a forest biologist and member of the Potawatomi Nation, writes, Indigenous peoples' languages are adept at expressing both this more generous distribution of consciousness and the entangled relationships between different beings. But just as our Western knowledge systems have excluded the possibility of knowers other than humans, so too have they marginalised these knowledges by dubbing them mythology, folklore or story. Again, who knows what we might be like if our claims on knowledge lost their selfishness.

It's a tough call, and not only because of our linguistic habits. Once you see that *other* others, not just *human* others, have a face, the responsibility to their lives becomes infinite. Every time you make them an object, every time you block out their faces, you betray them, and yourself as well. I have never got over something else Lévinas wrote. Sometimes, he admitted, we cannot bear that others have a face. We cannot tolerate what that would demand of us. So we want to murder them. It is just too much of a burden to remain alive to the truth that all of these other beings feel what it is like to be thirsty, or what it is like not to have the space to move, or experience the loss of the others they nourish and are nourished by. Sometimes, it is easier to kill them than to stay face to face.

But these are the poles: to answer the call to be infinitely responsible to others, or to kill them because we cannot bear that responsibility. And though extreme, there is something simple about poles. The path that seems most difficult to take is, perhaps, the possibility that lies before us. To acknowledge that we will inevitably fail in that infinite responsibility to all of those whose faces look out to this world; and still to remain present to their faces and respond, imperfectly.

gathering

Do you remember what it was like as a child to read, or have someone read you, a story in which other children (not unlike you) happened upon a surreptitious gateway that led to another, quite different, world? On one side, the side they used to live in, is the world where everything works as expected (although already there, you can feel their restiveness). On the other side, the one they step into, is a world where the old rules no longer apply. Species boundaries are muddled. The children can do and see things they could not do or see before. The laws of physics and the order of time acquiesce to desire, although not always the desires of the mystified children.

The first time we drove to this valley, it was as if all of these metaphors had come together. As you wind down from the top of the hill you climb as you drive out of the local town, you pass through open pastures – red flame trees, a bull in the shade – until the valley gradually folds in and tightens around you. Even in the middle of the day the canopy that the trees form overhead envelops you and subdues the light. The narrowing road leads you down to the river, which you cross once and then a second time. Except, that is, when one of the (historically) reliable deluges that inundates the upper reaches, cascading down the escarpments and drenching the whole valley, has turned the river into an impassable torrent, concealing the road. Once you cross, you start to climb again, past the original wooden farmhouse that is now stooped beneath wisteria vines and a giant grandiflora magnolia tree, through groves of tree ferns, and, depending on the time of year, oversized yellow flowers that look like pineapples, or pink, white and orange blossoms. At the top of the hill you round the corner and pass through the cupboard, the door, the garden, the pools, the rabbit hole, the looking glass. The valley opens before you.

Among the surest signs that you are entering a changed, curious world are the strange apparitions that you cannot but catch a glimpse of but also cannot quite make out as they flit across the road or disappear into the bush. It's not that they are insubstantial – they are actually fairly large if you include their long, almost translucent feathered tails, which are longer than the rest of them, butt to beak – but they move so curiously, and their form is so eccentric that most people are too busy doing a double take to fix a good look at them. And that is before you have heard them.

Before I came to live here, superb lyrebirds held for me the semi-mythic status they have for most people. We know them principally for their legendary talents as prodigious species-surpassing mimics. I say 'legendary' because the people who actually study them in the wild are dubious about the widespread belief that lyrebirds imitate not only other birds and bush creatures but also human technology: chainsaws, excavators, cameras. Lyrebirds who have been kept in captivity and so have lived their lives steeped in a human-made soundscape likely do, but for those who live among their more conventional neighbours, you would expect that these human-made sounds would make only rare, albeit remarkable, appearances in their calls.

Perhaps not, though. If the sounds of chainsaws and excavators have entered into lyrebirds' repertoires, that has to be because that is what they are hearing: the sound of the forest being cut down, dug up and carried away around them. I wonder how many of us who have found ourselves enthralled when listening to a recording of this elusive avian creature producing sounds that normally come out of heavy machinery have stopped and thought about what that machinery was doing to their worlds. I didn't until I wrote this.

If I am near the edge of the bush early in the morning or towards dusk I almost always hear them. I've come to know where they congregate, and make sure that my path takes me by at least some of those places. Even though their calls incorporate the sounds of other birds, once you become familiar with the lyrebird's sound you can pretty much always pick them out because others' sounds are punctuated by their own 'chorus'. And when they are not singing you might hear them scratching around in the rainforest understorey. Before I learned to recognise them they made such a racket that I assumed there must have been a wombat or wallaby under there. If I don't rouse on them first, or preemptively make my disapproval known, the dogs bound into the bush when they hear them, always hoping, but never managing, to catch one of them.

As we approached the summer months, still without rain, people in our community started to worry about the lyrebirds. We consider ourselves especially privileged to have their sounds form part of our background, to know that we need to drive slowly because most likely one or more will be on, or running off, the road. True, we still saw them around, but the drought was desiccating their habitat and there were fewer and fewer insects, frogs or small invertebrates for them to eat.

When the fires ripped up from the south towards us, and then turned towards the west, passing us by, and the lyrebirds who live here were spared, they became still more precious to us. We don't know how many of their cousins were killed and how many managed to survive the acute onslaught by finding their way to dams or rivers, or into wombat holes, as we know lyrebirds do. The work of tracking what happened to different species could not begin until the fire grounds were considered safe enough for researchers to enter, and within weeks the country went into lockdown in an effort to control the pandemic. So there is much that we will never know about what happened. We do know that for those who survived, the conditions of their lives might well have been shattered. Fire destroyed half of the habitat of the northern and central superb lyrebirds, and a third of the habitat of the subspecies that our lyrebirds belong to, the southern superb. When I watch the ones I am blessed to see run into the bush now, I wonder how many refugees are among them.

There is a part of the land that stretches from the other side of the river almost straight up to where the sheer rock escarpments rise in the west. Between the steep, rough terrain and the assortment of spiky, jagged or stinging bushes, trees and leaves, it is an inhospitable place for humans. But we have braved it, hesitatingly, a couple of times so we could get a window into what this world without us is like. You can vaguely make out a long-overgrown path that people used when they came up here to cut down and carry away the huge straight cedars that once grew here in abundance, or to fetch the cows that grazed here when this was dairy country. The last family who lived here, more than seventy years ago, would have used the trail to reach a small, now derelict cabin close to the top where the light falls on a high plateau. Along the path are vestiges of their various lives. A Land Rover with trees growing out where there were once windows; rusted remnants of old machinery half submerged in the earth; a tin shed with the remains of a picket fence still visible.

I imagine that there are some people who could recognise signs of the Aboriginal peoples who lived here, or who visited, perhaps to gather medicinal plants or collect food, to woo or to learn, until white colonial settlers decided that they wanted the land and its resources for themselves. I do not have the eyes to make those signs out.

On one occasion, as we made our way further into the bush, we spotted what looked to me like strange small stages, which is exactly what they were. About a metre wide and slightly raised, made of fine flattened dirt. I discovered that they were the courtship mounds male lyrebirds build to display themselves and sing their finest repertoire to prospective mates. Once you find a mound you soon stumble upon others. It seems a male lyrebird prefers to have a variety of staging platforms, presumably to maximise the likelihood that a female will make her way to one of them and he will have the opportunity to court her. When he does he will pass through his sequence of movements and styles of tail display – now fully fanned like a veil, now narrowed, and now over his head like a mohawk – each form accompanied by different songs or sounds. One of those sounds is so loud that, at ninety decibels from seven metres, we would lose our hearing if we were exposed to it on a regular basis.

Crouching near one of their mating mounds and imagining the song sequence, it was as if I had found my way back to the other side of a gateway to a world where I could see and hear what I had not been able to see or hear on the other side. No matter how many melodies I could hear elsewhere, the sequence sung by the bird who danced here would be strung together from the unique array of sounds that belong to *this* place.

We know that lyrebirds in different parts of Australia have distinctive songs, in part because they transmit melodies or refrains across generations to form their own sonic subcultures, in part because every place is unique. These lyrebirds, the collective whose territories lie within this place, are the gathering points of this distinctive sonic landscape. The tawny frog-mouth, the yellow-tailed black cockatoo, the fan-tailed cuckoo, the sacred kingfisher, the satin bowerbird, the yellow-throated scrubwren, the little wattlebird honeyeater, the olive-backed oriole, the rose robin. It is true, other members of those species and the others who live here might also be found elsewhere. But it is only here that you can find them in this assembly, sounding as they do against winds passing through these trees – the cabbage palms, the scented satinwood, the old-man banksia. Then again, on the far side of some other door, or through some other looking glass, are lyrebirds, also superb, who sing their own completely unique gatherings of life. So long as they do.

finitude

When I stand at the side window or on the porch facing north, my eyes either move up the valley to the escarpments, across to the now vast pecan tree that the man who lives in a cabin up the road planted thirty years ago, or down to the pond. I know the aspect well. When we first moved here my desk used to sit beneath that window. As I read, or wrote, or spoke on the phone, I'd occasionally find my gaze called by some feature of the tableau. When I was thinking, I'd often find my mind hovering just before the sheer rock exposed at the top of the escarpment to the north-west. Before, I used to love to travel, to place myself in front of the myriad wonders around this planet. Now I want to stay here, to take in the way that the movements of the light and the seasons create an endless array of scenes in this place.

Yesterday L called me to the porch to draw my eyes to a new sight. Anna, the sole remaining female Muscovy duck who lives here, was standing by the edge of the pond, watching over five mini black fuzzballs, each with a tiny patch of yellow like a bib, moving around her feet, never more than a few centimetres away. They must have hatched a few days ago and been huddling in the nest Anna built in the reeds at the edge of the pond. Perhaps this morning they became too restless for her to keep them in, or she decided it was time for them to come out into the world beyond the reeds.

When we moved here, the pond was populated by a community of wild wood ducks who flew in and out, as well as by a lone female Muscovy duck who lived here full-time. I assumed (incorrectly) that the name 'Muscovy' was a reference to Moscow, and so I called her Ivana. Several months later she was joined by a trio of large male Muscovies whom someone had dumped near the pond down the road. By then, I had learned that in fact Muscovies originate in Mexico and Central and South America. Perturbed by my geographic and cultural blunder, I played around with some Hispanic names, but they had firmly established themselves as the Russians, so I named them Ivan, Nikolai and Fyodor. The young males were rowdy, gregarious and appropriately menacing, but Ivana had a way about her, a gentleness and a poise. She retained her unparalleled status as original resident and the most respected member of the community.

In that first year, having always been within eyeshot, Ivana started to disappear for a couple of days at a time. On one of my walks exploring the land that was still largely unknown to me I eventually spotted her. She was just barely visible, but I heard her, protecting the nest she had created, crouched beneath the thick shrubs that now enveloped an abandoned piece of rusted machinery behind the barn. We had a brief feminist moment – or probably more accurately I wrote her into my feminist moment – enjoying the ingenuity and independence of her reproductive labour. The periods of her absences lengthened, until she did not come back at all. For as long as I could sustain it I insisted that we shouldn't give up on her. Early days, and I was still fully resistant to the reality of routine death among these beings I had come to live with. But eventually we had to accept that, most likely because she refused to abandon her nest, she had become the literal sitting duck.

With Ivana gone, the tenor of the conversation by the pond definitely went down a few notches. The guys now resorted to occasional matches of trying to drown each other, interspersed with longer, more low-key stretches of congregating in the shade or the sun, looking like they were involved in the duck equivalent of sharing stories about the old country or playing poker. On the long summer days they moved between the pecan tree, the Japanese maple, and the tree ferns that line the north side of the pond. Their names came to seem more and more fitting, even if I was the only one who insisted that it was Fyo and not Theo. Dostoevsky may not be widely read anymore but I was at least going to preserve his namesake.

During the ensuing years the composition of the crew shifted. We found Ivan down in the field below the house with a hole in his neck where a quoll had taken him. Few people even know that these small spotted Australian native carnivores exist, and until a few years ago just about everyone had concluded that the eastern quoll had become extinct on the mainland. But as people around here have been working to protect a corridor of habitat between the national parks, quolls have been returning to this rainforest. I have never seen one in the flesh but camera traps placed surreptitiously near the river captured images of them as they made their way down for a drink. Their numbers remain very low, and their robust establishment in this area – still a tenuous prospect – will take some years. Had the fire reached this place I can only assume this nascent return would have been cut off at the ankles. So when we found Ivan's body, I felt an ambivalence I was unfamiliar with when confronting a friend's death – dismay at the loss and his suffering, but gratitude that those almost-forever-gone creatures were finding a way back to live and kill on their land.

I still find myself in a state of emotional and intellectual conflict when an animal who lives here and with whom I have formed a relationship is eaten or killed. I have not learned – at an emotional level, I mean, and not just intellectually – to reconcile my grief at their death with my recognition that these movements of living and dying, killing and being killed are precisely the turns of the world I am trying to learn to live within. There are philosophers out there who think that ethics means minimising suffering and that this commitment calls on us humans to intervene in everyone and everything else's relationships. I appreciate what motivates them – the pain of witnessing suffering – but they seem to be basing their view of ethical action on the assumption that we humans occupy some privileged position from which we can come up with a calculation that measures the best possible arrangement of life. A humbler understanding of ethics would suggest that the very desire to make the world as we would have it is the root of the violence unfurling in front of our faces.

At the bottom of the large horse pasture, on a patch of ground perched at the top of a steep drop, and looking over the valley towards the escarpments, is where we bury the dead. Now that we have an excavator, L uses that to dig a hole if a large animal dies, but at first we dug the holes by hand. In our first summer, L and I dug graves big enough for two donkeys who died. The strain of the labour, my body wet with sweat and caked with dirt, a relief against the impossible grief of looking at their lifeless bodies. As time passes, it's not that I stop missing them, but I feel something like peace, or integrity, knowing that all of them are in their earth.

After Ivan was killed, Fyo and Niko remained alone for quite some time, becoming increasingly familiar and brazen. If they deemed that we were remiss in our obligation to feed them at the correct time of the day, they might come up on the porch or to the door where I now have my office, stomp around and make their distinctive heavy breathing sounds. It's a sight to see. On occasion they stand body to body, doing what looks like some type of ritual dance accompanied by a heavy-breathing chant. Sometime last year another seventeen-odd Muscovies were dumped near the pond down the road, and eight (presumably those who survived) came to live here. Fyo and Niko seemed nonplussed but generally amenable to their presence. Or so we thought until we were away one weekend and the friend who was here looking after everyone called in a state of anguish to say that one of the young males was floating dead in the pond, presumably Fyo and Niko's victim. By summer the crew comprised seven: one young male, whom I called Vronsky, and three females, Anna, Darya and Ekaterina (or Kitty). Enormously resented by Fyo and Niko, Vronsky (wisely) remained for the most part on his own, a safe distance from the young females.

In the days after we had evacuated the large (domestic) animals, I agonised over what to do with the ducks. Wood ducks are lithe, and I knew they could use their facility with flight to escape, even if they would likely be overtaken by smoke and exhaustion before they could find safety and rest.

But Muscovies are large and heavy, and even though they like to flap their wings and display their impressive wingspan it's really all performance. Sometimes, to make sure they get to the food before the others, Fyo and Niko fly from the other side of the pond to the top of the rise where I am throwing seeds, but that is about it. We decided we needed to try to get them out.

Switch, now, to the perspective of the ducks. To our minds we were taking them somewhere safe. But based on their responses it was pretty clear that our stealthily walking up to them, offering them food and then trying to put a sheet or a coat around them, meant something quite different to them. Certainly not safety. Who had the right to be deciding here? Respecting their autonomy seemed like a lame principle when they had no idea of the fire that was coming towards them. All options are bad options. Stay under the fern trees until the fire comes. Get stuffed into a cage in someone's backyard.

We eventually managed to rustle them into the little pen in the old milking shed, then into a cage and into the back of a car. The three girls, Fyo and Vronsky took shelter in a makeshift enclosure a friend had constructed in her backyard in the middle of town. Had the fire come to town she had a plan in place to take them along with her human family and dogs to the evacuation centre. I am not sure how the volunteers would have felt about that. After a day we had to move Fyo as it proved too dangerous to leave him and Vronsky in such close proximity to each other and to three women. In any case, he was much happier once he joined Niko in the little stall by the granny flat to which L and I had evacuated. The two of them huddled together in the middle of the small dark space and barely moved for the three days they were there.

When we brought them back to their pond they flew onto the island or into the water and danced. Irrespective of how sceptical you might be about our capacity for interspecies communication, there was no mistaking their sheer joy.

Some people might recoil at this concern for ducks when human life was at stake, and remains so at risk for people around the world – not only from climate-related disasters, but from the perennial burdens of poverty, ill health, insecurity and now from the pandemic. From this perspective, being able to show concern for ducks is no doubt a privilege. I don't want to be insensitive to that. From another perspective, though, it is a simple matter of justice. We (if we can, just for these purposes, think of humanity in collective terms) created the conditions of their vulnerability; are we not then called upon to protect them from its ravages as best we can? There is a black hole of ethical impossibility in questions about who of the living beings on this planet ought to get priority of care. With their trolley problems and ticking time bomb scenarios, professional ethicists have gone to great lengths to game out the correct choice when the perfect, loss-free choice is beyond reach. But every choice in the actual world, and not in an imaginary construction of the world, is a tangle of diverse attachments, values, commitments, needs, available options and temporalities. Responsibility for our carbon-dense atmosphere falls unevenly across humans, and its deathly fallout spreads even less equally over all of us who live here. At this point some of us have a certain luxury in our choices of actions and perhaps the time to think through, together, how to make the choices we will have to make. Down the track we will not.

As summer softened, Darya and Kitty began to disappear, as Ivana had, although from the direction they came back when they spotted me near the large bin where we keep their food it looked like their nests were over in the rainforest by the road where the lyrebirds hang out. The periods between their returns lengthened until they too did not return. Anna found a spot deep in the reeds in the pond, and continued to come out every few days. On the occasions when she did emerge, I chased Fyo, Niko and Vronsky away (no easy task) to make sure she ate well. The sisterhood continues. A few times we thought she had gone for good, but then she would reappear.

When I saw the ducklings, I ran out and took photos of them to send to some of the people in my life who are finding it hard to crawl out of hopelessness. Even those who were not directly touched by the fires are now living with the realities of COVID-19. It's difficult to know what to say to people who feel the weight of the times in their bodies. One friend wrote back to express her wonder at the ducklings' capacity just to *be*, and be completely oblivious to the crumbling world around them. In truth, with the snakes and large birds and foxes and quolls who live here, I'm not sure how long their lives will be. It is tempting to take them into the enclosure we created as an emergency ward in the old milking sheds, where they would be safe from those dangers. But this morning I watched their mama stand on the pontoon that L built, supervising them as they moved in a small circle in the water beneath her. I am trying to learn this new dance, moving between the dangers we have imposed, and vulnerabilities that are intrinsic to the lives we might still respect. How to love amid grave danger, as these other animals and trees already must.

after all

When almost everything save what we needed to sit on, eat on and put on was gone from the house, two pieces of art remained. It wasn't that we could not live without them, nor that we were prepared to sacrifice them if the house burnt. They were just too cumbersome to take down and pack into the moving truck, so they stayed where they were. They hung alone on the wall right in front of the wooden table where L and I sat, checked in on fire developments on our computers, wrote lists, ruminated, and fell silent.

One of the pieces is a large steel disc, cut so that the light that passes through the stencilled patterns forms a counterpart shadow on the wall behind it. The other is made of 484 small sculpted pewter birds, threaded together with pieces of wire to form a huge curtain that falls to just above the wooden floorboards. When the wind comes through the windows that look out onto the duck pond, the curtain sways gently and you can hear a faint clink of the birds moving.

The house did not burn, and these two pieces of art now live once again among the others that have come home. Summer is coming to an end. It seems that the rains that have fallen during these last weeks will afford us a few months protection from new fires. During these coming months we will not procrastinate over building a bunker, as we did before when we believed that the time between us and danger stretched out indefinitely. The focus of the world's eyes have already shifted from this place, and our fires, to a pandemic. Were I writing this at another moment, they might have shifted to another place and its fires; or another and its typhoons; or another and its floods; or another and its hurricanes; or another and its extinctions; or another and its ruined ecosystems. There is no premium on catastrophe these days. Ours too will pass into memory.

Someone else will find themselves amid those losses as I was in the midst of mine. This time I will try not to regard them as if through a lens that turns them into an image. As if it is not really happening. As if, when I turn my attention away, they will not still be there, or they will no longer be there.

There is so much we do not pay attention to, including what is right before our faces. It was only after weeks of watching the light move through the two remaining artworks, and the many moods move through me, that I woke up to the significance of their titles. One is called *Teardrop*. The other: *After all it is always someone else who dies.*

world

caring

When we first brought Jimmy home I wrote an article about his trauma and the gravity of his sadness. I wrote for the public (and not just for myself) because I wanted there to be some record of what had happened to him and to Katy. For them to not just disappear among the numbers, and for at least an intimation of the reality of the impact of these fires of the Anthropocene on beings other than humans to begin to enter our human consciousness.

What I did not expect was the effect that Jimmy, or my attempt to portray him, would have on people who read about him. He provoked responses in the form of letters sent to me expressing people's grief and anger over what he and others like him had experienced, wanting to know how he now was, requesting updates, asking to come to visit him. Two women asked me to seek his permission to start giving him remote reiki. Another sent a box filled with bottles of Rescue Remedy and other healing treatments. Another sent homeopathic medicines. Someone gifted him a session with a psychic healer. Others advised me on supplements to give him – charcoal to soak up the toxins, vitamin C, probiotics, barley broth, corn silk. The care his story engendered took L and me aback. It also took us right back to the form of the life we had imagined we were creating when we moved to this place, before that life was overwhelmed by the fires. Here was care organised around neither species distinctions, nor around the idea of the individual. The fire's path knew no boundaries, and although we humans certainly provided ourselves far more protection against its ravages than we did for other earth beings, perhaps in the end our experience of the fire also burnt through some of the borders that we perennially place around ourselves.

For many weeks – what felt like a lifetime – it was not clear that Jimmy was going to make it. Even long after the fire had passed, the radiant heat, the dehydration he experienced in the days after, the charred material he ingested, the loss of Katy now become permanent – forms of violence and terror I cannot possibly know and cannot imagine – combined and sank into his body. At the lowest point he did not eat, he did not drink, and he did not pee. His eyes seemed empty and grey. He vomited green bile. He turned away from us.

The gifts that people had wanted to pour over him paled against whatever had already entered his body and was taking root in his guts and his kidneys. On the worst of the searing hot days when we thought we might lose him we were left with no choice but to put our faith in his capacity to take himself to the coolest parts of his world and to rest his being down into the earth. If we were lucky, he might remain still enough for the wet towels we placed over his back to stay on his body. At a certain point Jimmy's life was Jimmy's call.

And then he turned. He climbed, slowly, up the hill from his forested world and walked out into the field and ate green grass. I was so overwrought that I ran over to his wallow, stuck my arms deep into the water and covered (myself and) him with cool mud. In the next days he began to eat the bowls of organic rice with lentils or adzuki beans L cooked for him. Apples. Bananas he especially loved. Cabbages and broccoli he hated. He stuck his nose in the water and swashed it around. He drank. He was back.

But he was a different pig. Or perhaps we were a different human-pig relation. At his meals we hung close, infused with ridiculous joy at the sight and sounds of him eating. My phone is full of little clips I filmed of those first days of his head in the bowl, slurping up his noodles. When he was done I rubbed his belly and he lay down beside us. I stroked his face and talked to him while L brushed him with the horse brush we keep hanging on a post near the gate to his world. Jimmy chatted in a low voice. Whatever fear we had held in the face of a being who occurred to us as huge and 'foreign' evaporated. Whatever hesitation he had held in the face of beings who occurred to him as perhaps unpredictable and sometimes anxious evaporated. We mirrored each other's transformation like dancers. In place of the hesitations that had always lurked around us emerged intimacies – emotional and physical – that were surprising for all three of us.

All of this raises some thorny questions about relationships among humans and other animals. One that I have been contemplating concerns what you might call 'the politics of care'. What does it mean to care across species lines, against a background of a history of domestication that is itself fraught with domination? The easiest answer, at least as an abstract idea, is to let them be: to withdraw our presence and leave spaces where other lives can flourish in our absence. A fantasy of wilderness, immunised from the toxicity of humans, whose lives seem incompatible with others' flourishing. I have little doubt that creating spaces for some other beings to live far from us is critical if their lives are to flourish. But the singularity of the earth, now pervaded with the artefacts of human life, also means that there is no longer any place where others could live entirely free from the effects that humans are having on them. Even those animals and ecosystems we call wild, and that live, in theory, independent of us, are now infused with the atmosphere we (or perhaps more accurately *some* of us) have made. We, the ones who claimed to be bringing progress to the whole world, are ubiquitous.

Far more difficult, it seems to me, is the challenge of working out how to live together in ways that are both ethical and realistic. There can be no pretending that vast asymmetries don't exist, nor any denying the power we humans wield. But that does not preclude acknowledging *our* interdependence, our finitude, and our embeddedness in a world where there are myriad ways of being alive that we may encounter and also may never be able to understand. Far more difficult is giving up on the fantasy that Eden or its equivalent can be restored, and being present to a planet that both bears our stamp everywhere and always exceeds us. A planet in peril. And us in trouble.

I have come to doubt the idea that if only we could identify the grand plan for recovery we would then be able to construct a world to realise it; that if only we could ascertain the correct principles we could then follow them and attain something like justice or peace or safety. My guess is that it is going to be far messier than that. More a matter of forging the track than finding it. Definitely more a matter of collaboration than pioneering.

The others with whom I share this home, and with whom I shared the weeks of the fires, have already taught me a few things – the donkeys' attentiveness to each other's signals and their shared responsiveness to the messages they discern from the other beings around them, the smells, the changing light. And Jimmy, generous being that he is, has come up to me on a few summer days and wiped the mud that he covers his own body with on my bare white arms, as if to say, 'Hey, girlfriend, you are going to get sunburnt.'

A brilliant answer to the puzzle I'd been trying to solve of how to protect my white human body from the harshness of the sun without poisoning the river with sunscreen.

I am surely not the only one who would benefit from hours of quietly lying under the trees instead of locking myself in an office and writing about those same trees' marvellous capacity to lower temperatures and cortisol levels. It might not be a bad idea for those of us also dealing with ecological grief and the trauma of the recent and unfolding devastations to visit the cool of the places Jimmy built himself to heal.

I know we crave a better answer than that. A formula. A credo. But I'm guessing the reason those answers promise comfort is because they reflect back what we already know. A mirror, not a face.

changing

While they were burning and then after they eased, conversations across the world were saturated with the Australian fires: their ferocity, their expanse, the devastation they caused, not only to people but to the Australian ecosystems and native animals that hold a type of mythic quality for many. Images circulated of a kangaroo joey's body soldered to a fence; of burnt-out gum forests stretching out beyond the reach of the camera; of koalas in humidicribs; of birds' bodies, feathers dishevelled, strewn on ash-covered beaches. It was not that we did not know that climate catastrophes were on the horizon, but for many of us, especially those whose voices dominate public space, that horizon had seemed to hover at a distance sufficiently remote for us to gaze at it passively and continue to live our lives. Part of the shock was that it happened to this place, both exotic and familiar. And, let's face it, predominantly white. Part of the shock was the rapidity with which it came upon us. A fire flare is precisely the right image. The ground can be parched, the trees desiccated and the atmospheric temperature soaring, but the flame itself goes from nothing to all-consuming in a matter of moments.

In the weeks after, it felt like there was nothing else to speak about. Conferences were organised, compensation schemes to support people who had lost their homes and livelihoods were set up, volunteer groups mushroomed across the country, creating makeshift feeding and watering stations for surviving animals. Then something else happened. The urgent conversations about the fires and what they meant went quiet, the heartfelt attention to people left bereft turned elsewhere, the desperate need to save the surviving animals dissipated. As I write, the conversations across the world are saturated with the pandemic: the deaths it is bringing, the economic havoc that our attempts to protect ourselves is wreaking, the prospect of future pandemics. Now, across the planet, billions of people are in their homes, save the people for whom working outside their homes is essential to support their own lives and the lives of everyone who is at home. And there are those who have no home to be in.

In one sense, it seems that the pandemic has obscured everything that the fires made apparent. Yet, like the fires, the pandemic grew in the soil of humans' rancorous relationship with the earth and other earth beings. Our incursion into every space, our disruption of every set of relationships, our felt entitlement to extract, construct and belch out what we don't desire is now the source of the fires making parts of the planet uninhabitable and of the diseases that have crossed over into our own species, ironically rendering us impotent.

So here we are again, where there seems to be nothing else to talk about. Each catastrophe is a genuine index of very real injustices and sufferings. But there is a risk that our total absorption in the crisis of the moment will obscure the larger shifts that are afoot. Perhaps as you read this you are still in the midst of the pandemic. Perhaps you are reading this from a world changed otherwise, in which another crisis has torn down the apparently solid structures of what we care about and how we live. I sense that the tidal patterns within which the particular waves of the next crisis and the one after are now forming, but they are amorphous and remote. From here there is no way of predicting what you will be worried about, or working on, or trying to deal with as you read this. I wrote earlier that safety was one of the casualties of our time. So too is stability or predictability.

That change happens gradually has been one of the greatest psychic buffers against our recognising the reality of what is happening with the climate. We simply cannot imagine that climate variations could be so wild as to undo our lives. We mistook it for weather, which has long mimicked it, fluctuating in ways that would have us change the clothes we wear outside. That change happens slowly has also been one of the greatest impediments to our believing that we could effect the transformations we will need to make if we are to have a part in consciously altering how the future will unfold. Among us, there are vast differences in privilege and vulnerability – differences given by wealth, race, ability, gender, I could go on and still leave some out. But we have all enjoyed the privilege of the Holocene. Stable, hospitable. Giving us summers that follow springs and precede autumns.

Now the error this privilege has engendered, the idea that it must be thus, stares us in the face. Changes are altering our worlds at a pace few of us could have imagined. They carry on their backs a multitude of global shifts, both related and distinct, unravelling what we thought was sutured in for good.

When we think about how we know the world and ourselves, most likely we do not even notice the rhythms we take for granted. The lengths of days, the movements of seasons and the pace of change are the background, not the feature. But as the beat gathers pace it is becoming impossible not to notice it. As it quickens, the distinctions between the sections of the orchestra – the part we call nature, the part we call culture, the part we call environment, the part we call society, the part we call human and the part we call everything else – are becoming more difficult to hear. The tempo quickens; the distinctions fade.

killing

When I was growing up, one of my parents' favourite albums was a live recording of a Pete Seeger concert called *We Shall Overcome*. On it was his rendition of a Bob Dylan song called 'Who Killed Davey Moore?' Pete's voice, imploring an answer to that question, would ring out from the record player in the living room and across the house.

The song explores the question of who bore responsibility for the death of an African American boxer who was killed in the ring when he was just thirty years old. Each verse begins with the refrain, 'Who killed Davey Moore?' In the verse that follows, some group or individual associated with his life and death – the coach, the crowd, the manager, the gambling man, the boxing writer, the other fighter – gives their answer. Each, in turn, responds 'Not I', and explains that they cannot rightfully be accused of killing Davey Moore. They were just doing what it is that they do: going to the fight, organising the fight, writing about the fight, throwing the punches, and so on. And, of course, they are each telling the truth. Or a truth of sorts.

Even to the child I was then, the song conveyed the miserable inadequacy of reducing responsibility to something uniquely borne by individuals who malevolently commit bad actions. The repetitive beat of justification and exculpation left no doubt in that little girl that even those who could swear they had not committed the actual act of killing, and certainly had no intention to kill, had their hands deep in his death. This was no tragedy, as if he had been inexplicably struck down by the fates, like a figure who falls on the stage in a Sophocles play. They all killed Davey Moore.

Who killed Katy? Who killed the 3 billion animals we estimate died as a result of these fires? What about the trees, the grasses, the insects, the microbes, the fungi? What about the people? What about our faith in the future? What about summertime?

Their deaths, and the threats they face in the

future, are no tragedy. We know what killed them, and we know what is threatening the lives of all of us who remain. But our knowing lacks language, lacks law, lacks a path to action.

This is not the first time we have stood in the face of crimes we could not name. At the end of the Second World War, as the full extent of the devastation of the Shoah became apparent, Raphael Lemkin, a Polish Jew whose entire family had been killed, pulled himself from a grief we can barely contemplate to try to find ways to prevent the killing he had witnessed from ever happening again. In facing that gargantuan task, he realised that he could not even get started as long as there was no name for the distinctive crime that had been committed: the murder of a people. So, he set as his first goal giving a name to the crime, and then to convince the world to use this name and thereby come to recognise it as a crime. He achieved both. Today the term genocide is part of our lingua franca, and although we have not yet learned how to prevent genocide few would argue that it is anything less than a scourge on the earth. Today, no one calls genocide a tragedy. No one says, it's unspeakably terrible, but after all, it's no one's fault.

Lemkin's greatest aspiration, and one he barely had a chance to commence before he died, was to develop the laws, build the institutions and create the understandings that would have the world not only name and condemn genocide but actually go about ensuring that it did not happen. Among the many reasons that might explain our continued failure to realise his aspiration is the Davey Moore problem. True, the specific murders of the individuals who belong to the murdered people can be traced to specific killers, but the roots of genocide, the causes that perpetuate it through history, burrow far deeper into our politics, our economics, our cultures, and our ways of making sense of who we, and who others, are.

What then might we make of this killing of our age? What word might we give to it? This time, the suffix *-cide*, or killing, cannot be delimited. In these pages I have written of the death of animals, of trees, of ecosystems and of summertime. Others have written and spoken of the deaths of animals and places they treasure, of people they know and have loved, of oceanscapes, of insects, of living beings we cannot see but know are disappearing, of entire species; the death of their sense of being at peace in the world. In the future they may be writing of the death of civilisations.

Already, as parts of the planet become too hot for humans to continue to live there, or too volatile for them to live safely, civilisations woven from millennia of connection to place are being mourned by people who carry away stories of worlds being left behind. The ubiquity of the climate catastrophes unfolding – not only here, where I felt the fire, but across the planet – can perhaps give us some inkling of how deep we are all in this. The killing has no boundaries. Everything is within its sights. Perhaps the term could be *omnicide*. The killing of all. Not just all humans, as if humans were the only beings that could be murdered. All beings.

What would it take for us to stop this killing? How do we even begin to wrap our heads around its enormity? How do we trace the complex roots of responsibility into all the places where they are dug deep into our politics, into our economics, into the ways we understand ourselves and everyone and everything else with whom we share this earth? Can we learn to tell new, far-reaching stories about responsibility? Do we have the capacity to put our names to stories that both recognise the unevenness of culpability and its concentration in particular types of practices and arrangements – and, yes, also in particular people and groups of people – and at the same time, to acknowledge the ways in which we are all implicated?

And if we can learn to tell these types of complex stories, how do we go about wresting our lives and ways of life back from those pathological practices and malignant institutions? How do we learn to understand ourselves and everyone else, human and other-than-human, in ways that will help us extricate ourselves and those who will come after us from omnicidal ways of being human? How do we attach ourselves to stories that have the power to woo us away from the spells of progress and the logics of extraction and violence that have legitimated the killing?

Shining an accusatory light on an evil killer is both easy and relatively satisfying. It drives the script of the tales in which we absorb ourselves as we retreat from a world become too much. Far more unnerving is to recognise that the killing is the secretion of this human world just doing what it is that it does. Day in day out. This killing is not an event but a condition.

Pete Seeger sang for the sixties, in the hope that the people who heard him might step out from passivity and take on the violence and injustice infecting their world. If we were now to sing, 'Who killed everything?', would we fill the verses with a new version of, 'Not I, not I, not I'?

Or could we now, while we still can, sing and then answer, 'I, I, I'?

living

In the morning, when Jimmy comes over to wait for us to bring him his breakfast, these days he does a variation of the dance that he and Katy used to do, running up and down the fence line. We called it 'La Cage aux folles' because they almost seemed to have choreographed their turns and passes. Only now it is not Katy with whom he is dancing, but a small copper-coloured girl who came to share a life with him. I named her Penelope, or more colloquially Penny, so that Jimmy might always have a safe shore to return to.

That he has been able to find his way into life has been a blessing. He has been graced with the character, the good luck and the intensity of care to bring him out of the trauma and loss to a place where he is able not only to live but to find friendship, and again take pleasure in a world that had turned violent on him.

The ending of this story is, though, only the ending of a story. Or at least the ending for now, because there is still story to come. And whatever transpires later does not annul what came before. Nor does it stand in for the stories and the endings of all the others, human and other-than-human, who have, however they have, made their way, with their losses, their scars and their memories on into life or into death.

Does a story of survival and recovery offer us redemption? Or does it at least spare us the burden of feeling condemned for the crime of omnicide? I cannot deny that when I see Jimmy and Penny running in the rain-soaked field there is a softness in my body quite different from the cocktail of anxiety, anger, fear and grief that tends to pulse through me when I think about our world. They bring me comfort.

Isaac used to say, 'Where there is life there is hope.' Because you know a little of him, you know that the 'life' of which he was speaking could not *but* have been pervaded with the reality of death. More than that, with the reality that death may always be crouching on the horizon. The hope to which he alluded was no consoling fantasy. He knew, and I now know, that where there is life there is the presence of death. Where there is hope there is mourning. They are entwined. I have come to believe that if there ever was an age of primary-colour emotions, it is over. But probably there never was such an age.

Sometimes when I look over towards where Jimmy lives I forget that Katy is not there. In the fraction of a second before the timeframe of the real reasserts itself, I imagine that I can see her there. Sometimes when Penny waits, calmly, as she tends to, for me to put her food bowl over the fence, I recollect how anxiously Katy chewed the wire while she was waiting for me to organise myself. I can still feel how much it pained me to see that even then she could not be free from a past that lived on in her body. I am still alive to my incapacity to alleviate her suffering. I sense the taste of the metal in my mouth.

I do not resent that it is now me who is haunted by Katy. Katy, the terror that surrounded her when she died, and right behind her, the billions of others and the terrors that surrounded them when they died, have altered the quality of my relationship with the future. I look to it with neither hope nor dread. Both are far too abstract and too remote to actually *feel* like anything at all. Rather, I find myself tethered to it, as if I am woven into a braid of all of the different attachments and loves that I have for all of the different beings who have this thing called life. As long as they do, and then still after they do.

remembering

Some words come to mind. They are the ones people from my culture say to each other when someone who was loved dies.

May their memory be a blessing.

Let the words not stop there.

May their memory be a blessing and a curse.

acknowledgements

Once you become alive to the multitude of relations that nourish you and make it possible for you to write, and of their reach well beyond the ones you have with other humans, you also realise that acknowledgements ought to be near infinite. Given the confines of the page, I limit myself to acknowledging just some of you. The land that has held me through this writing, the rainforest that has transformed from brittle back to cool and dank, the trees that have changed from summer to autumn to winter and now into spring, the birds whose songs kept me company and brought me joy when I felt dark, to all of the animals with whom I live and who never cease to remind me of your myriad ways of experiencing and communicating the world.

Turning now to the humans, my first thanks are to my friend and colleague Scott Stephens at the ABC. Beyond publishing three of the original pieces that formed the embryo of this book, you provided the listening into which I felt able to write in all of the rawness of the moment. Thank you also for reading and commenting on multiple drafts of this book, and along with your comments, always sending back an image of myself worth striving towards.

It was in the Sydney Environment Institute that I landed as I began to appreciate the true scope of ethics and politics, and the demand they placed on me to work in the world of environmental thinking and acting. Thank you for welcoming and supporting me Michelle St Anne, David Schlosberg, and all of the SEI crew. I also want to acknowledge the SEI for publishing some of the early material about Jimmy that made its way into this book.

The members of the Multispecies Justice collective have created an intellectual and emotional home for me as I have grown my ideas about what it means to live as part of a multispecies world. Thank you especially Sophie Chao, Dalia Nasar, Astrida Neimanis, Thom van Dooren, Dinesh Wadiwel, Anik Waldow and Christine Winter. Thank you Gemma Viney and Genevieve Wright for what you do to make our collective sing.

I shared the first draft of *Summertime* with the women in my writing group who have been a source of wisdom, sustenance and humour these last years. You offered me invaluable ideas that made this a far better book than it would have been without you. Thank you Barbara Caine, Helen Groth, Clare Monagle, Julia Kindt, Tess Lea and Glenda Sluga.

To my best friend and thought partner, Moira Gatens, thank you for being my teacher and continuing to be a reader in whom I have complete trust. As always, you provided me with keen insights into the text and the perspective of readers.

I am fortunate to have a number of people in my life with whom I am in an ongoing conversation about what it means to live and to live ethically in a climate-changing world. Our conversations have sunk into my own thinking and are woven through this book. Thank you Arielle De Bono, Andrea Durbach, Oliver Kunz, Sacha McDonald Shaw, Hugo McDonald Shaw, Laura McManus, Simon Perrett, Josh Salzman and Richard Sherwin.

Although they were not directly involved in my writing this book, I also want to acknowledge the people who played a critical role in our lives throughout the period of the fires, many of whom made it possible for us to care for the animals as the threat approached. In my local community, thank you Naomi Barrett, Wayne Barrett, Hilary Brickhill, Susan Locke, Sassi El Husseini,

Di Ellis, Michael Ellis, Jen Rootham, and all of the people in the horse rescue network who came the moment I called. My special thanks to Heather Lord. Thank you to the friends and family who were so mindful in holding us as we tried to hold ourselves together, Toni Baumann, David Celermajer, Noirin Celermajer, Chris De Bono, Maryanne Kovaks, Chris Lawton, Lydia Loberthal, Karl Maton, Ruti Teitel and Julie Vulcan. Thank you to the extended network of folks who were intimately involved in caring for Jimmy, and who have been my teachers and partners in the world of animals, especially Melissa Boyde, Colin Dayan, pattrice jones and Catherine Schuetze. Thank you to the animal sanctuary network, especially Charlie Jackson-Martin, Penny Cameron, Melanie Ellis, Naty Guerrero-Diaz and Judy Woods. A very special thanks to the people whose hearts Jimmy touched and who sent healing remedies and thoughts to him in those weeks when he was deciding if he was going to live. My deepest acknowledgement and gratitude to you Marylin Mills; your love for animals, the constancy of your care and your courage are a perennial inspiration.

The team at Penguin Random House Australia has been brilliant and I am deeply grateful for your support, your encouragement, your advice, your expertise and your dedication. Until I worked with you, I had not imagined how wonderful it would feel to be part of a book-creating team.

Thank you especially to my publisher, Nikki Christer, who saw *Summertime* before I did and who has been an invaluable conversation partner in bringing it to fruition. Thank you Genevieve Buzo, for your thoughtful editing, and to all the folks at Penguin who were responsible for what it takes to make a book and get it into the hands of readers. Thank you Richard Flanagan, for the gift of the name, and Dan Spielman for seeing Rilke in Jimmy and Katy as they lay, still together, in the sun.

I am very grateful to the photographer Adam Stevenson for noticing and capturing the moment of the kookaburra looking out at the fire-ravaged landscape and his generosity in allowing me to use it for the cover of *Summertime.*

All of the experiences written here were refracted through endless conversations and silences, then tossed back and forth and wrought into words until they were ready to rest for good on the page. That is you, L.

about the author

A professor at the University of Sydney, Danielle Celermajer has written two previous books, *The Prevention of Torture* and *The Sins of the Nation and the Ritual of Apologies*, for Cambridge University Press, the top publisher in her field. She has edited several other books for Bloomsbury, Stanford University Press and Routledge. She is a regular on ABC Radio National's *The Minefield* with Waleed Aly and Scott Stephens and *The Philosopher's Zone*. She has also written for the *Sydney Morning Herald*, the *Guardian* and the Conversation.